Life and Death

Other New and Forthcoming Titles from
HACKETT
READINGS IN PHILOSOPHY

Life and Death

Edited, with an Introduction, by
Jonathan Westphal
and
Carl Levenson
Idaho State University

Hackett Publishing Company, Inc.
Indianapolis/Cambridge
1993

Copyright © 1993 by Hackett Publishing Company, Inc.

Printed in the United States of America

07   06   05   04   03   02   3   4   5   6   7

Text design by Dan Kirklin

For further information, please address

Hackett Publishing Company, Inc.
P.O. Box 44937
Indianapolis, Indiana 46244-0937

Library of Congress Cataloging-in-Publication Data

Life and death/edited and introduced by Jonathan Westphal & Carl
Levenson.
       p. cm. (Readings in philosophy)
      ISBN 0-87220-209-7 (cloth: alk. paper)
      ISBN 0-87220-208-9 (pbk.: alk. paper)
      1. Life. 2. Death. I. Westphal, Jonathan, 1951–
II. Levenson, Carl Avren, 1949–   . III. Series.
BD431.L4164   1993
128—dc20   93-11501
                                                     CIP

The paper used in this publication meets the minimum requirements of
American National Standard for Information Sciences—Permanence of
Paper for Printed Library Materials, ANSI Z39.48-1984.
∞

Contents

    We Can Call God," from *Notebooks 1914–1916*   146

17. Leo Nikolaevich Tolstoy, "The Fundamental Contradiction
    of Human Life" and "The Fear of Death Is Only a
    Confession of the Unsolved Contradiction of Life,"
    from *Life*   152

18. Simone Weil, "Detachment," from *Gravity and Grace*   162

19. William Shakespeare, "Fear No More. ..." from
    Cymbeline   166

    Some Suggested Further Reading   168

    Index   171

Introduction

1. The first formulation of the philosophical problem of the meaning of life in this anthology is Plato's. In his *Euthydemus* he causes Socrates, a participant in the dialogue, to say that the aim of life is happiness. Yet Socrates points out that the good things in life cannot of themselves make us happy, because whether or not they do depends on the use we make of them, and it is easy enough to imagine circumstances in which we would make very bad use of them. So we might welcome the suggestion in the dialogue that there could be an *art* of using things correctly. Whoever possessed this art would infallibly use all things in a way that promoted happiness. But then every art would need another, to make the right use of it, and this second art would need a third, and so on. This suggests that what is needed is an all-encompassing and self-sustaining art, an art which, "to use the language of Aeschylus, sits at the helm of the state, governing all things, ruling all things, and making all things useful." But the participants in the dialogue fail to find this "royal art," as they call the ultimate knowledge they are seeking. With this failure, the conversation ends.

In his dialogue about the death of Socrates, the *Phaedo*, Plato has found a method for making sure that one makes the right use of all things. He gives it the name of "the practice of death," meaning a rehearsal of death, or achieving a deathlike state in life. The loss of the material world can be stimulated through a certain detachment from it before the final coming of death. But why should we want to invite our own death? Socrates explains that the anticipatory experience of death makes the standards one ought to have lived by stand out with a special clarity and "concentrates the mind" most wonderfully. At the same time it purifies us of the weaknesses which have made it difficult to live rightly, and the meanings of life, the so-called Platonic Forms or Ideas, appear beyond the present life.

2. Aristotle declares in our brief selection from the *Nicomachean Ethics* that Plato's royal art is political science. The highest good at which it aims must be happiness, because only it has the right logical characteristics. It alone is complete and self-sufficient, and its application requires no further justification, a claim made later in this volume

by Moritz Schlick for *play* (Selection 14). This view of the good is down-to-earth and sensible, though perhaps not divine.

    3. The transcendental Platonic context reappears in our selection from St. Augustine's *Confessions*, but it is about the death of someone else, not our own death, and how this affects the way we see the meaning of our life. St. Augustine is writing about grief and loss, and these too can concentrate the mind in a special way on the question of the value of life. He does not actually use our modern phrase "the meaning of life," but he is describing the loss of his life's most central value, a "very dear friend." When this friend dies, the center of St. Augustine's life becomes death:

> My heart was black with grief. Whatever I looked upon had the air of death. My native place was a prison-house and my home a strange unhappiness. The things we had done together became sheer torment without him. My eyes were restless looking for him, but he was not there. I hated all places because he was not in them. They could not say "He will come soon" as they would in his life when he was absent. . . . I had no delight but in tears, for tears had taken the place my friend had held in the love of my heart.

    Idolatry might be defined as an attempt to set up something finite as the central meaning of life. Lovers and friends, job, possessions, even clothes or physical appearance are all temptations to idolatry. "What folly," Augustine sighs, "to love a man as something more than human." For all idols are bound to collapse in the end.
    Only God, according to St. Augustine, provides ultimate meaning in life. Only God can gather everything into one meaningful whole that cannot be destroyed by death. St. Augustine makes a famous analogy between this "gathering up" and the succession of words in a sentence, all contributing to a single meaning. As the speaker is to a sentence, so God is to human life. As the speaker causes words to fit together, so God causes events to fit together. But if one were to identify the meaning of life with one of its parts (a friend, for example, or a task, or a possession, etc.), it would be as if one had identified the meaning of a spoken sentence with some single word in the sentence, and then complained that, since the chosen word had passed, the whole sentence could have no meaning. (Of course the meaning of life, for St. Augustine, is contained in the figure of Christ. Christ is like a word that contains the whole point of a sentence. But then

Christ for St. Augustine never ceases to be present. He does not "pass away" like other beings.)

St. Augustine's analogy between God and a speaker is actually more than an analogy. God creates the world by speaking it, and all creation signifies the meanings contained in Him. The single "Word" is God's very being. For St. Augustine, then, God is the meaning of life. Though we may think the meaning of life is *more* shadowy and abstract than the events of life, in fact it is more alive than anything else. God is life itself.

4. In this same tradition, the chapter "Concerning Life" from Dionysius the Areopagite's *The Divine Names* begins:

> Now let us praise Eternal Life from which comes Life itself and all, and from which is imparted to all things, however they participate in life, the life appropriate to each.

All creatures are living insofar as they partake of Eternal Life. And by life, Dionysius means not only the biographical sense as Augustine is using it in the *Confessions*, but also life in the full biological sense, the life of the function and growth of organisms.

5. The selection from St. Thomas Aquinas also emphasizes that life is the origin not only of organic life, but of all things. And it is the end of all things as well. This ultimate happiness, as St. Thomas calls it in Chapter 37 of the *Summa contra Gentiles*, is the contemplation or understanding of God. "The knowledge of God therefore is the last end of all human study and activity." St. Thomas arrives at this conclusion by claiming that only in the contemplation of God's truth can an activity and its aim coincide. Only the contemplation of God is in itself valuable. The value of each thing depends on its use, and therefore on the value of some further thing. But it is only God beyond which there is nothing further. This is the basis of St. Thomas's version of Plato's "royal art" or "practice of death."

It might be objected that final happiness is in "the goods of the body." Thomas's answer is that the soul is better than the body. He also rejects honors and glory, riches, power, and acts of virtue. Could the soul's activity of contemplation apart from these provide a satisfactory meaning to life? Some might think it too limited and perhaps too intellectual a life. This would overlook how special a form of contemplation St. Thomas has in mind and how unique its object is as he conceives it. To appreciate this fully, however, one would need to go beyond our selection to the center of Thomas's theology, where he discusses what God is.

6. If we gather together what St. Augustine, Dionysius, and St. Thomas say about God as the end or meaning of life and what Plato says about "the royal art," we can understand how catastrophic it must have been for the understanding of the meaning of life when the conviction of God's presence was diminished in the centuries before Nietzsche wrote his parable of the madman, which contains the famous slogan "God is dead." This is more than a statement of atheism, that God does not exist. Nietzsche even says that we have "killed" God. What these unsettling paradoxes mean is unclear, but at least they express a sense of loss and responsibility, as a simple denial of God's existence would not. And Nietzsche also says that, as a result of our having "killed" God, we confront a world without meaning:

> Where were we standing when we unchained the earth from the sun? Whither is it going now? Whither are *we* going? Away from all suns? Are we not plunging continually? Backwards, forwards, sidewards in all directions? Is there any up or down left? . . . Is not night and more night coming on all the while?

In another mood, Nietzsche rejoices in the death of God, because he thinks that the God of the Christianity is a repressive figure who prevents us from living life fully. Here Nietzsche has fixed on just one strand in Christianity, the ascetic one. There are others. But his implication is that there is no life beyond the present one. So Nietzsche offers the bizarre notion that everything happens over and over again. He seems to be saying that reality is stuck, like a gramophone needle, but he also has in mind the idea that we can find infinite value in the present and thus will its eternal repetition.

7. What is the present moment like, without a meaning beyond itself? In Sartre's novel *Nausea*, the hero, Rocquentin, has a vision which is, so to say, the structural opposite of Plato's. Sartre describes a scene in the park in its sheer existence, or "facticity"—a scene which is entirely without meaning. Until his vision, Rocquentin had not noticed the existence of things in their superabundant but festering

life, because he had concentrated on the meaning and use they had
for him in his orderly human world.

> And then all of a sudden, there it was, clear as day. Existence had suddenly
> unveiled itself. It had lost the look of an abstract category. It was the very
> paste of things. . . . Or rather the root, the park gates, the bench, the sparse
> grass, all that had vanished: the diversity of things, their individuality, were
> only an appearance, a veneer. This veneer had melted, leaving soft, mon-
> strous masses, all in disorder—naked, in a frightful, obscene nakedness.

8. The idea that life is absurd is commonly associated with the
name of Albert Camus, the novelist. His vision of an absurd world is
less subjective and esoteric than Sartre's, and it is about the meaninglessness of daily life. Camus asks what its final value is, saying that it
is not going anywhere except to death. The mind requires a final
meaning, order, beauty, and goodness, but in the end the world refuses
to oblige. We are left with the meaningless routine of everyday life.
According to Camus, we keep hoping that the world will satisfy us
and grant us some kind of secure happiness. But we are constantly
disappointed.

Camus sums up this tragic estimate of the sense of life in the
celebrated *Myth of Sisyphus*. Sisyphus, a figure from Greek mythology,
has been condemned by the gods to an eternity rolling a rock up a
hill, watching it roll to the bottom, and then having to roll it to the top
again. Camus is commonly taken to have interpreted the myth in a
very negative sense. Yet he has Sisyphus finally able to scorn his fate
and achieve a noble happiness. According to Camus,

> Sisyphus teaches that higher fidelity that negates the gods and raises rocks.
> . . . This universe henceforth without a master seems to him neither sterile
> nor futile. Each atom of that stone, each mineral flake of that night-filled
> mountain, in itself forms a world. The struggle itself toward the heights is
> enough to fill a man's heart. One must imagine Sisyphus happy.

And just as Camus describes so well the "divorce" between the needs
of the mind or soul and the fulfillments of the world, so, in another,
less complex mood, in our selection from *Nuptials*, he describes the
union of the mind with the beauty and sense the world occasionally
offers.

9. Sartre writes about existence as "soft" and "naked"; Camus describes a "divorce" from the world and a "nuptial union" with it. These images are clearly sexual, and in them the image of the feminine enters the discussion of the meaning of life. Our selection from *The Second Sex*, by Simone de Beauvoir, a friend of Camus's and a long-time associate and close friend of Sartre's, makes this connection explicit. She says that, through the ages, Woman has come to symbolize Nature, the flesh, the womb, and Life itself. Transcendence and meaning, on the other hand, are felt, in these associations, to be masculine. So since meaning is masculine and life is feminine, for de Beauvoir, the question of the meaning of life takes its character from a prior understanding of the relationship between the sexes. De Beauvoir is able to evoke in her writing much of the power and beauty of the traditional view of women, but at the same time she believes that it has distorted the nature of both sexes.

10–11. The American philosopher Thomas Nagel defines absurdity formally. In his essay on "The Absurd" he defines an absurd situation as one in which our view of what is going on diverges from reality. In this sense our lives must be absurd because the seriousness with which we take them conflicts with the ever-present possibility of doubt about the values which ground the seriousness. Nagel ends his piece with some remarks about Camus, saying that if "there is no reason to believe that anything matters, then that doesn't matter either, and we can approach our absurd lives with irony instead of heroism or despair."

12. In "Nothing Matters," the moral philosopher Richard Hare describes an eighteen-year-old guest in his house who had been over-taken by a powerful sense that "nothing matters," as a result of reading Camus's novel *The Stranger*. In this novel, Mersault, the hero, shouts, "Nothing matters!" at a priest who wants him to confess and receive absolution. Hare manages to get his young friend to agree that mattering is mattering *to* someone, that there is no such thing as the mattering of something to no one. Mattering is not like the emission of an invisible radiation. If one thought it was, one might try to detect it and, failing to find it anywhere, conclude that nothing matters. The error here would be a misconception of "mattering." As Hare puts it,

My friend had not understood that the function of the word "matters" is to express concern; he had thought that mattering was something (some activity or process) that things did, rather like chattering; as if the sentence "My wife matters to me" were similar in logical function to the sentence "My wife chatters to me."

13. Hare's piece does raise the question of what the question "What is the meaning of life?" actually means. For John Wisdom, it does not have much to do with mattering and concern. Meaning is rather a matter of context and pattern. This does of course raise the *Euthydemus* problem about where the wider pattern gets its meaning. Wisdom asks us to imagine missing the beginning and end of a play. We might ask, of what we have seen, "What does it mean?" But, he says, if we think this question asks for a single phrase, rather than a whole narrative, we may conclude that the question lacks meaning, since there could be no such formula. This is hardly surprising, though, since many things of interest cannot be reduced to a formula. What one finds so hateful or so lovable in another person is Wisdom's example.

14. A more clearly "this-worldly" discussion is A. J. Ayer's "The Meaning of Life," which he wrote shortly before his death in 1989. Ayer was a very well known opponent of religion, so it is interesting to see how much of his essay is about the implications of the religion he rejects. His own solution is that there is no larger context of meaning for our lives. "Evidently there is no general answer to the question what constitutes a meaningful life." This does not seem to have troubled Ayer. His view is one of people getting on with their lives and pursuing the things that they personally value.

15. The next pieces bring together many themes in this anthology. With Moritz Schlick, we are back to Socrates' original question. The difficulty is that the goods or values which are attained in life gain their value from the purpose they serve. But then this purpose gains its value from a further purpose, and the further purpose from yet another purpose, and so on, it seems, forever. Schlick says that

No, life means movement and action, and if we wish to find a meaning in it we must seek for *activities* which carry their own purpose and value within them independently of any extraneous goals. . . . There really are such activities. To be consistent, we must call them *play*, since that is the name for free, purposeless action. . . .

The free purposeless action in which Schlick says meaning originates belongs typically to childhood and youth. So Schlick is able to say, "I assert the proposition that *the meaning of life is youth*."

16. Wittgenstein offers a similar thought. The meaning of life can be found only in the present ("A man lives eternally if he lives only in the present") but Wittgenstein also says something Schlick would never agree with, that the meaning of life does *not* lie in the world. "The meaning of life . . . we can call God," he writes, in apparent agreement with St. Augustine.

17. Wittgenstein also says that "Fear in the face of death is the best sign of a false, i.e. a bad, life," and this comes directly from Tolstoy, whom Wittgenstein was reading at the time he wrote the *Notebooks*. One of Tolstoy's formulations of this thought is that "The fear of death is only a confession of the unsolved contradiction of life." Another is that

> People who fear death fear it because it represents emptiness and darkness to them; but they behold emptiness and darkness because they do not see life.

18. Like Schlick, Wittgenstein, and Tolstoy, Simone Weil thinks that purposes are incompatible with an ultimately meaningful life. For Schlick the way to purposelessness is through the self-fulfillment of youthful play. For Weil it lies in the opposite direction, in the sacrifice of self. This sacrifice consists of the total detachment of our desires from any possible gain, including, remarkably, even spiritual gain. "We have to fix our will on the void," which is "fuller than all fullness," for "God fills the void."

19. We end our collection with some lines from Shakespeare's *Cymbeline*.

> Fear no more the heat o' th' sun,
>   Nor the furious winter's rages;
> Thou thy worldly task hast done,
>   Home art gone, and ta'en thy wages:
> Golden lads and girls all must,
> As chimney-sweepers, come to dust.

In these lines Shakespeare seems to be saying no more than that death brings an end to the anxieties of life. Yet this absence of worldly tasks is presented so hauntingly that we seem to recognize in it all of life's meaning. It remains unclear whether the "home" to which we go after the "worldly task" is merely the dust to which the "golden lads and girls" all must come, or something more.

Acknowledgments

Plato, from *Phaedo*, transl. by G.M.A. Grube, 1980, Hackett Publishing Company, Inc.

Aristotle, from *Nicomachean Ethics*, transl. by Terence Irwin, Hackett Publishing Company, Inc. Copyright © 1985 by Terence Irwin.

Jean-Paul Sartre, *Nausea*. Copyright © 1964 by New Directions Publishing Corporation. All rights reserved. Reprinted by permission of New Directions Publishing Corporation.

From *Lyrical and Critical Essays* by Albert Camus, trans., E. C. Kennedy. Copyright © 1967 by Hamish Hamilton Ltd. and Alfred A. Knopf, Inc. Reprinted by permission of Alfred A. Knopf, Inc.

From *The Myth of Sisypus and Other Essays* by Albert Camus, trans., J. O'Brien. Copyright © 1985 by Alfred A. Knopf, Inc. Reprinted by permission of the publisher.

From *The Second Sex*, by Simone De Beauvoir, trans. H. M. Parshley. Copyright 1952 by Alfred A. Knopf, Inc. Reprinted by permission of the publisher.

Excerpts from Thomas Nagel, "The Absurd," 1971, *Journal of Philosophy* lxiii 20, by permission of the *Journal of Philosophy*.

"Is Life Absurd?" from *Philosophy*, 1990, with permission by Cambridge University Press.

From *Applications of Moral Philosophy*, by Richard Hare. Copyright The Macmillan Press Ltd. Reprinted with permission of the publisher.

Excerpts from John Wisdom, *Paradox and Discovery*, 1962, Basil Blackwell. Reprinted with permission of the publisher.

From *The Meaning of Life*, by A. J. Ayer, Weidenfeld & Nicolson. Reprinted with permission of the publisher.

Excerpts from Moritz Schlick, "On the Meaning of Life," from *Philosophical Papers*, vol. II, translated by Peter Heath, edited by Henk L. Mulder and Barbara F. B. Van De Velde Schlick, 1979, Kluwer Academic Publishers. Reprinted by permission of Kluwer Academic Publishers.

Excerpts from Ludwig Wittgenstein, *Notebooks 1914–1916*, 1979, Basil Blackwell. Reprinted by permission of Basil Blackwell and the Wittgenstein Trustees.

Excerpts from Simone Weil, *Gravity and Grace*, © The Putnam Publishing Group. Reprinted with permission of the publisher.

Augustine, from *Confessions*, trans. by Frank Sheed, 1993, Hackett Publishing Co., Inc.

Plato,
"On the Aim of Life,"
from the *Euthydemus*,
"On the Practice of Death,"
from the *Phaedo*

It has been said by Whitehead that all subsequent philosophy is merely a series of footnotes to Plato, Greek philosopher and poet, and founder of the Academy at Athens. Plato wrote a series of dialogues in which Socrates, his teacher, is the most important speaker. In the following text, taken from the Euthydemus, *Socrates discusses, with a pupil named Cleinias, the purpose of human life.*

Euthydemus

Son of Axiochus, answer me:

Do all men wish to do well? Or is this question one of the ridiculous ones I was afraid of just now? I suppose it is stupid even to raise such a question, since there could hardly be a man who would not wish to do well.

No, there is no such person, said Cleinias.

Well then, I said, the next question is, since we wish to do well, how are we to do so? Would it be through having many good things? Or is this question still more simple-minded than the other, since this must obviously be the case too?

He agreed.

Well then, what kinds of existing things are good for us? Or perhaps this isn't a difficult question and we don't need an important personage

Plato, from *Euthydemus*, trans. Rosamond Kent Sprague, Indianapolis and Cambridge: Hackett, 1993.

to supply the answer because everybody would tell us that to be rich is a good—isn't that so?

Very much so, he said.

And so with being healthy, and handsome, and having a sufficient supply of the other things the body needs?

He agreed.

And again, it is clear that noble birth, and power, and honor in one's country are goods.

Well then, if every workman had all the materials necessary for his particular job but never used them, would he do well by reason of possessing all the things a workman requires? For instance, if a carpenter were provided with all his tools and plenty of wood but never did any carpentry, could he be said to benefit from their possession?

Not at all, he said.

Well then, if a man had money and all the good things we were mentioning just now but made no use of them, would he be happy as a result of having these good things?

Clearly not, Socrates.

So it seems, I said, that the man who means to be happy must not only have such goods but must use them too, or else there is no advantage in having them.

You are right.

Then are these two things, the possession of good things and the use of them, enough to make a man happy, Cleinias?

They seem so to me, at any rate.

If, I said, he uses them rightly, or if he does not?

If he uses them rightly.

Well spoken, I said. Now I suppose there is more harm done if someone uses a thing wrongly than if he lets it alone—in the first instance there is evil, but in the second neither evil nor good. Or isn't this what we maintain?

He agreed that it was.

Then what comes next? In working and using wood there is surely nothing else that brings about right use except the knowledge of carpentry, is there?

Certainly not.

And, again, I suppose that in making utensils, it is knowledge that produces the right method.

He agreed.

And also, I said, with regard to using the goods we mentioned first—

wealth and health and beauty—was it knowledge that ruled and directed our conduct in relation to the right use of all such things as these, or some other thing?

It was knowledge, he said.

Then knowledge seems to provide men not only with good fortune but also with well-doing, in every case of possession or action.

He agreed.

Then in heaven's name, I said, is there any advantage in other possessions without good sense and wisdom? Would a man with no sense profit more if he possessed and did much or if he possessed and did little? Look at it this way: if he did less, would he not make fewer mistakes; and if he made fewer mistakes, would he not do less badly; and if he did less badly, would he not be less miserable?

Yes, indeed, he said.

And in which case would one do less, if one were poor or if one were rich?

Poor, he said.

And if one were weak or strong?

Weak.

If one were held in honor or in dishonor?

In dishonor.

And if one were brave and self-controlled would one do less, or if one were a coward?

A coward.

Then the same would be true if one were lazy rather than industrious?

He agreed.

And slow rather than quick, and dull of sight and hearing rather than keen?

We agreed with each other on all points of this sort.

So, to sum up, Cleinias, I said, it seems likely that with respect to all the things we called good in the beginning, the correct account is not that in themselves they are good by nature, but rather as follows: if ignorance controls them, they are greater evils than their opposites, to the extent that they are more capable of complying with a bad master; but if good sense and wisdom are in control, they are greater goods. In themselves, however, neither sort is of any value.

It seems, he said, to be just as you say.

Then what is the result of our conversation? Isn't it that, of the other things, no one of them is either good or bad, but of these two, wisdom is good and ignorance bad?

He agreed.

Then let us consider what follows: since we all wish to be happy, and since we appear to become so by using things and using them rightly, and since knowledge was the source of rightness and good fortune, it seems to be necessary that every man should prepare himself by every means to become as wise as possible—or isn't this the case?

Yes, it is, he said.

And for a man who thinks he ought to get this from his father much more than money, and not only from his father but also from his guardians and friends (especially those of his city and elsewhere who claim to be his lovers), and who begs and beseeches them to give him some wisdom, there is nothing shameful, Cleinias, nor disgraceful if, for the sake of this, he should become the servant or the slave of a lover or of any man, being willing to perform any honorable service in his desire to become wise. Or don't you think so? I said.

You seem to me to be absolutely right, said he.

But only if wisdom can be taught, Cleinias, I said, and does not come to men of its own accord. This point still remains for us to investigate and is not yet settled between you and me.

As far as I am concerned, Socrates, he said, I think it can be taught.

I was pleased and said, I like the way you talk, my fine fellow, and you have done me a good turn by relieving me of a long investigation of this very point, whether or not wisdom can be taught. Now then, since you believe both that it can be taught and that it is the only existing thing which makes a man happy and fortunate, surely you would agree that it is necessary to love wisdom and you mean to do this yourself. . . .

So, Cleinias, I said, remind me where we left off. As far as I can remember it was just about at the point where we finally agreed that it was necessary to love wisdom, wasn't it?

Yes, he said.

Now the love of wisdom, or philosophy, is the acquisition of knowledge, isn't that so? I said.

Yes, he said.

Well, what sort of knowledge would we acquire if we went about it in the right way? Isn't the answer simply this, that it would be one which will benefit us?

Certainly, he said.

And would it benefit us in any way if we knew how to go about and discover where in the earth the greatest quantities of gold are buried?

Perhaps, he said.

But earlier, I said, we gave a thorough demonstration of the point that even if all the gold in the world should be ours with no trouble and without digging for it, we should be no better off—no, not even if we knew how to make stones into gold would the knowledge be worth anything. For unless we also knew how to use the gold, there appeared to be no value in it. Or don't you remember? I said.

Yes, I remember very well, he said.

Nor does there seem to be any value in any other sort of knowledge which knows how to make things, whether money making or medicine or any other such thing, unless it knows how to use what it makes—isn't this the case?

He agreed.

And again, if there exists the knowledge of how to make men immortal, but without the knowledge of how to use this immortality, there seems to be no value in it, if we are to conclude anything from what has already been settled.

We agreed on all this.

Then what we need, my fair friend, I said, is a kind of knowledge which combines making and knowing how to use the thing which it makes.

So it appears, he said.

Then it seems not at all needful for us to become lyre makers and skilled in some such knowledge as that. For there the art which makes is one thing and that which uses is another; they are quite distinct although they deal with the same thing. There is a great difference between lyre making and lyre playing, isn't there?

He agreed.

And it is equally obvious that we stand in no need of the art of flute playing, since this is another of the same kind.

He said yes.

Seriously then, said I, if we were to learn the art of writing speeches, is this the art which we would have to get if we are going to be happy?

I don't think so, said Cleinias in answer.

On what ground do you say this? I asked.

Well, he said, I notice that certain speech writers have no idea of how to use the particular speeches they themselves have written, in the same way that the lyre makers have no idea of how to use their lyres. And in the former case too, there are other people who are capable of using what the speech writers have composed but are themselves unable to write. So it is clear that in regard to speeches too, there is one art of making and another of using.

You seem to me, I said, to have sufficient ground for stating that the art of speech writing is not the one a man would be happy if he acquired. And yet it was in this connection that I expected the very knowledge we have been seeking all this time would put in an appearance. Because, as far as I am concerned, whenever I have any contact with these same men who write speeches, they strike me as being persons of surpassing wisdom, Cleinias; and this art of theirs seems to me something marvelous and lofty. Though after all there is nothing remarkable in this, since it is part of the enchanters' art and but slightly inferior to it. For the enchanters' art consists in charming vipers and spiders and scorpions and other wild things, and in curing diseases, while the other art consists in charming and persuading the members of juries and assemblies and other sorts of crowds. Or do you have some other notion of it? I said.

No, he said, it seems to me to be just as you say.

Where should we turn next, then? I asked. To which one of the arts?

I find myself at a loss, he said.

But I think I have discovered it, said I.

Which one is it? said Cleinias.

The art of generalship seems to me, I said, to be the one which, more than any other, a man would be happy if he acquired.

It doesn't seem so to me, he said.

How is that? said I.

Well, this art is a kind of man hunting.

What then? I said.

No art of actual hunting, he said, extends any further than pursuing and capturing: whenever the hunters catch what they are pursuing they are incapable of using it, but they and the fishermen hand over their prey to the cooks. And again, geometers and astronomers and calculators (who are hunters too, in a way, for none of these make their diagrams; they simply discover those which already exist), since they themselves have no idea of how to use their prey but only how to hunt it, hand over the task of using their discoveries to the dialecticians— at least, those of them do so who are not completely senseless.

Well done, I said, most handsome and clever Cleinias! And is this really the case?

Very much so. And the same is true of the generals, he said. Whenever they capture some city, or a camp, they hand it over to the statesmen—for they themselves have no idea of how to use the things they have captured—just in the same way, I imagine, that quail hunters hand theirs over to quail keepers. So, he said, if we are in need of that art which will itself know how to use what it acquires through making or capturing, and if it is an art of this sort which will make us happy, then, he said, we must look for some other art besides that of generalship.

Crito. What do you mean, Socrates? Did that boy utter all this?*

Socrates. You're not convinced of it, Crito?

Crito. Good heavens no! Because, in my opinion, if he spoke like that, he needs no education, either from Euthydemus or anyone else.

Socrates. Dear me, then perhaps after all it was Ctesippus who said this, and I am getting absent-minded.

Crito. Not my idea of Ctesippus!

Socrates. But I'm sure of one thing at least, that it was neither Euthydemus nor Dionysodorus who said it. Do you suppose, my good Crito, that some superior being was there and uttered these things—because I am positive I heard them.

Crito. Yes, by heaven, Socrates, I certainly think it was some superior being, very much so. But after this did you still go on looking for the art? And did you find the one you were looking for or not?

Socrates. Find it, my dear man—I should think not! We were really quite ridiculous—just like children running after crested larks; we kept thinking we were about to catch each one of the knowledges, but they always got away. So why should I recount the whole story? When we got to the kingly art and were giving it a thorough inspection to see whether it might be the one which both provided and created happiness, just there we got into a sort of labyrinth: when we thought we had come to the end, we turned round again and reappeared practically at the beginning of our search in just as much trouble as when we started out.

Crito. And how did this come about, Socrates?

Socrates. I shall tell you. We had the idea that the statesman's art and the kingly art were the same.

Crito. And then what?

* Socrates' old friend Crito has been listening to the story about the conversation with Cleinias. When the story becomes implausible, Crito raises an objection.

Socrates. It was due to this art that generalship and the others handed
over the management of the products of which they themselves were
the craftsmen, as if this art alone knew how to use them. It seemed
clear to us that this was the art we were looking for, and that it was
the cause of right action in the state, and, to use the language of
Aeschylus, that this art alone sits at the helm of the state, governing
all things, ruling all things, and making all things useful.

Crito. And wasn't your idea a good one, Socrates?

Socrates. You will form an opinion, Crito, if you like to hear what
happened to us next. We took up the question once again in somewhat
this fashion: Well, does the kingly art, which rules everything, produce
some result for us, or not? Certainly it does, we said to each other.
Wouldn't you say so too, Crito?

Crito. Yes, I would.

Socrates. Then what would you say its result was? For instance, if I
should ask you what result does medicine produce, when it rules over
all the things in its control, would you not say that this result was
health?

Crito. Yes, I would.

Socrates. And what about your own art of farming, when it rules over
all the things in its control—what result does it produce? Wouldn't
you say that it provides us with nourishment from the earth?

Crito. Yes, I would.

Socrates. Now what about the kingly art; when it rules over all the
things in its control—what does it produce? Perhaps you won't find
the answer quite so easy in this case.

Crito. No, I certainly don't, Socrates.

Socrates. Nor did we, Crito. But you are aware of this point at least,
that if this is to be the art we are looking for, it must be something
useful.

Crito. Yes indeed.

Socrates. And it certainly must provide us with something good?

Crito. Necessarily, Socrates.

Socrates. And Cleinias and I of course agreed that nothing is good
except some sort of knowledge.

Crito. Yes, you said that.

Socrates. Then the other results which a person might attribute to
the statesman's art—and these, of course, would be numerous, as for
instance, making the citizens rich and free and not disturbed by fac-
tion—all these appeared to be neither good nor evil; but this art had

to make them wise and to provide them with a share of knowledge if it was to be the one that benefited them and made them happy.

Crito. True enough. So you agreed on this for the moment at any rate, according to your account.

Socrates. And does the kingly art make men wise and good?

Crito. Why not, Socrates?

Socrates. But does it make all people good, and in every respect? And is it the art which conveys every sort of knowledge, shoe making and carpentry and all the rest?

Crito. I don't think so, Socrates.

Socrates. Then what knowledge does it convey? And what use are we to make of it? It must not be the producer of any of those results which are neither good nor bad, but it must convey a knowledge which is none other than itself. Now shall we try to say what in the world this is, and what use we are to make of it? Is it agreeable to you if we say it is that by which we shall make others good?

Crito. Certainly.

Socrates. And in what respect will they be good and in what respect useful, as far as we are concerned? Or shall we go on to say that they will make others good and that these others will do the same to still others? But in what conceivable way they are good is in no way apparent to us, especially since we have discredited what are said to be the results of the statesman's art. It is altogether a case of the proverbial "Corinthus, son of Zeus"; and, as I was saying, we are in just as great difficulties as ever, or even worse, when it comes to finding out what that knowledge is which will make us happy.

Crito. Mercy on us, Socrates, you seem to have got yourselves into a frightful tangle.

Our next text is from the Phaedo, *the dialogue about the death of Socrates. Socrates explains that the purpose of human life is achieved through a "practice of death."*

Phaedo

I want to make my argument before you, my judges, as to why I think that a man who has truly spent his life in philosophy is probably

Plato, from the *Phaedo*, trans. by G.M.A. Grube, 1980, Hackett Publishing Company, Inc.

right to be of good cheer in the face of death and to be very hopeful that after death he will attain the greatest blessings yonder. I will try to tell you, Simmias and Cebes, how this may be so. I am afraid that other people do not realize that the one aim of those who practise philosophy in the proper manner is to practise for dying and death. Now if this is true, it would be strange indeed if they were eager for this all their lives and then resent it when what they have wanted and practised for a long time comes upon them.

Simmias laughed and said: By Zeus, Socrates, you made me laugh, through I was in no laughing mood just now. I think that the majority, on hearing this, will think that it describes the philosophers very well, and our people in Thebes would thoroughly agree that philosophers are nearly dead and that the majority of men is well aware that they deserve to be.

And they would be telling the truth, Simmias, except for their being aware. They are not aware of the way true philosophers are nearly dead, nor of the way they deserve to be, nor of the sort of death they deserve. But never mind them, he said, let us talk among ourselves. Do we believe that there is such a thing as death?

Certainly, said Simmias.

Is it anything else than the separation of the soul from the body? Do we believe that death is this, namely, that the body comes to be separated by itself apart from the soul, and the soul comes to be separated by itself apart from the body? Is death anything else than that?

No, that is what it is, he said.

Consider then, my good sir, whether you share my opinion, for this will lead us to a better knowledge of what we are investigating. Do you think it is the part of a philosopher to be concerned with such so-called pleasures as those of food and drink?

By no means.

What about the pleasures of sex?

Not at all.

What of the other pleasures concerned with the service of the body? Do you think such a man prizes them greatly, the acquisition of distinguished clothes and shoes and the other bodily ornaments? Do you think he values these or despises them, except in so far as one cannot do without them?

I think the true philosopher despises them.

Do you not think, he said, that in general such a man's concern is not with the body but that, as far as he can, he turns away from the body towards the soul?

I do.

So in the first place, such things show clearly that the philosopher more than other men frees the soul from association with the body as much as possible?

Apparently.

A man who finds no pleasure in such things and has no part in them is thought by the majority not to deserve to live and to be close to death; the man, that is, who does not care for the pleasures of the body.

What you say is certainly true.

Then what about the actual acquiring of knowledge? Is the body an obstacle when one associates it in the search for knowledge? I mean, for example, do men find any truth in sight or hearing, or are not even the poets[1] forever telling us that we do not see or hear anything accurately, and surely if those two physical senses are not clear or precise, our other senses can hardly be accurate, as they are all inferior to these. Do you not think so?

I certainly do, he said.

When then, he asked, does the soul grasp the truth? For whenever it attempts to examine anything with the body, it is clearly deceived by it.

True.

Is it not in reasoning if anywhere that any reality becomes clear to the soul?

Yes.

And indeed the soul reasons best when none of these senses troubles it, neither hearing nor sight, nor pain nor pleasure, but when it is most by itself, taking leave of the body and as far as possible having no contact or association with it in its search for reality.

That is so.

And it is then that the soul of the philosopher most disdains the body, flees from it and seeks to be by itself?

It appears so.

---

1. "Even the poets" because poetry concerns itself with the world of sense and appeals to the passions and emotions of the lowest part of the soul in the *Republic* (595a ff.), whereas in the *Phaedo* passions and emotions are attributed to the body.

What about the following, Simmias? Do we say that there is such a thing as the Just itself, or not?

We do say so, by Zeus.

And the Beautiful, and the Good?

Of course.

And have you ever seen any of these things with your eyes?

In no way, he said.

Or have you ever grasped them with any of your bodily senses? I am speaking of all things such as Size, Health, Strength and, in a word, the reality of all other things, that which each of them essentially is. Is what is most true in them contemplated through the body, or is this the position: whoever of us prepares himself best and most accurately to grasp that thing itself which he is investigating will come closest to the knowledge of it?

Obviously.

Then he will do this most perfectly who approaches the object with thought alone, without associating any sight with his thought, or dragging in any sense perception with his reasoning, but who, using pure thought alone, tries to track down each reality pure and by itself, freeing himself as far as possible from eyes and ears, and in a word, from the whole body, because the body confuses the soul and does not allow it to acquire truth and wisdom whenever it is associated with it. Will not that man reach reality, Simmias, if anyone does?

What you say, said Simmias, is indeed true.

All these things will necessarily make the true philosophers believe and say to each other something like this: "There is likely to be something such as a path to guide us out of our confusion, because as long as we have a body and our soul is fused with such an evil we shall never adequately attain what we desire, which we affirm to be the truth. The body keeps us busy in a thousand ways because of its need for nurture. Moreover, if certain diseases befall it, they impede our search for the truth. It fills us with wants, desires, fears, all sorts of illusions and much nonsense, so that, as it is said, in truth and in fact no thought of any kind ever comes to us from the body. Only the body and its desires cause war, civil discord and battles, for all wars are due to the desire to acquire wealth, and it is the body and the care of it, to which we are enslaved, which compel us to acquire wealth, and all this makes us too busy to practise philosophy. Worst of all, if we do get some respite from it and turn to some investigation, everywhere in our investigations the body is present and makes for confusion and fear, so that it prevents us from seeing the truth.

"It really has been shown to us that, if we are ever to have pure knowledge, we must escape from the body and observe matters in themselves with the soul by itself. It seems likely that we shall, only then, when we are dead, attain that which we desire and of which we claim to be lovers, namely, wisdom, as our argument shows, not while we live; for if it is impossible to attain any pure knowledge with the body, then one of two things is true: either we can never attain knowledge or we can do so after death. Then and not before, the soul is by itself apart from the body. While we live, we shall be closest to knowledge if we refrain as much as possible from association with the body or join with it more than we must, if we are not infected with its nature but purify ourselves from it until the god himself frees us. In this way we shall escape the contamination of the body's folly; we shall be likely to be in the company of people of the same kind, and by our own efforts we shall know all that is pure, which is presumably the truth, for it is not permitted to the impure to attain the pure."

Such are the things, Simmias, that all those who love learning in the proper manner must say to one another and believe. Or do you not think so?

I certainly do, Socrates.

And if this is true, my friend, said Socrates, there is good hope that on arriving where I am going, if anywhere, I shall acquire what has been our chief preoccupation in our past life, so that the journey that is now ordered for me is full of good hope, as it is also for any other man who believes that his mind has been prepared and, as it were, purified.

It certainly is, said Simmias.

And does purification not turn out to be what we mentioned in our argument some time ago, namely, to separate the soul as far as possible from the body and accustom it to gather itself and collect itself out of every part of the body and to dwell by itself as far as it can both now and in the future, freed, as it were, from the bonds of the body?

Certainly, he said.

And that freedom and separation of the soul from the body is called death?

That is altogether so.

It is only those who practice philosophy in the right way, we

say, who always most want to free the soul; and this release and
separation of the soul from the body is the preoccupation of the philosophers?

So it appears.

Therefore, as I said at the beginning, it would be ridiculous for a
man to train himself in life to live in a state as close to death as possible,
and then to resent it when it comes?

Ridiculous, of course.

In fact, Simmias, he said, those who practise philosophy in the right
way are in training for dying and they fear death least of all men.
Consider it from this point of view: if they are altogether estranged
from the body and desire to have their soul by itself, would it not be
quite absurd for them to be afraid and resentful when this happens?
If they did not gladly set out for a place, where, on arrival, they may
hope to attain that for which they had yearned during their lifetime,
that is, wisdom, and where they would be rid of the presence of that
from which they are estranged?

Many men, at the death of their lovers, wives or sons, were willing
to go to the underworld, driven by the hope of seeing there those for
whose company they longed, and being with them. Will then a true
lover of wisdom, who has a similar hope and knows that he will never
find it to any extent except in Hades, be resentful of dying and not
gladly undertake the journey thither? One must surely think so, my
friend, if he is a true philosopher, for he is firmly convinced that he
will not find pure knowledge anywhere except there. And if this is so,
then, as I said just now, would it not be highly unreasonable for such
a man to fear death?

It certainly would, by Zeus, he said.

Then you have sufficient indication, he said, that any man whom
you see resenting death was not a lover of wisdom but a lover of the
body, and also a lover of wealth or of honours, either or both.

It is certainly as you say.

And, Simmias, he said, does not what is called courage belong
especially to men of this disposition?

Most certainly.

And the quality of moderation which even the majority call by that
name, that is, not to get swept off one's feet by one's passions, but to
treat them with disdain and orderliness, is this not suited only to those
who most of all despise the body and live the life of philosophy?

Necessarily so, he said.

If you are willing to reflect on the courage and moderation of other people, you will find them strange.

In what way, Socrates?

You know that they all consider death a great evil?

Definitely, he said.

And the brave among them face death, when they do, for fear of greater evils?

That is so.

Therefore, it is fear and terror that make all men brave, except the philosophers. Yet it is illogical to be brave through fear and cowardice.

It certainly is.

What of the moderate among them? Is their experience not similar? Is it licence of a kind that makes them moderate? We say this is impossible, yet their experience of this unsophisticated moderation turns out to be similar: they fear to be deprived of other pleasures which they desire, so they keep away from some pleasures because they are overcome by others. Now to be mastered by pleasure is what they call licence, but what happens to them is that they master certain pleasures because they are mastered by others. This is like what we mentioned just now, that in some way it is a kind of licence that has made them moderate.

That seems likely.

My good Simmias, I fear this is not the right exchange to attain virtue, to exchange pleasures for pleasures, pains for pains and fears for fears, the greater for the less like coins, but that the only valid currency for which all these things should be exchanged is wisdom. With this we have real courage and moderation and justice and, in a word, true virtue, with wisdom, whether pleasures and fears and all such things be present or absent. Exchanged for one another without wisdom such virtue is only an illusory appearance of virtue; it is in fact fit for slaves, without soundness or truth, whereas, in truth, moderation and courage and justice are a purging away of all such things, and wisdom itself is a kind of cleansing or purification. It is likely that those who established the mystic rites for us were not inferior persons but were speaking in riddles long ago when they said that whoever arrives in the underworld uninitiated and unsanctified will wallow in the mire, whereas he who arrives there purified and initiated will dwell with the gods. There are indeed, as those concerned with the mysteries say, many who carry the thyrsus but the Bacchants are few.[2] These latter are, in my opinion, no other than those who have practised philosophy in the right way. I have in my life left nothing undone in order to be counted among these as far as possible, as I have been eager to be in every way. Whether my eagerness was right and we accomplished anything we shall, I think, know for certain in a short time, god willing, on arriving yonder.

This is my defence, Simmias and Cebes, that I am likely to be right to leave you and my masters here without resentment or complaint, believing that there, as here, I shall find good matters and good friends. If my defence is more convincing to you than to the Athenian jury, it will be well.

2. That is, the true worshippers of Dionysus, as opposed to those who only carry the external symbols of his worship.

2

Aristotle, "Happiness Makes a Life Choiceworthy," from the *Nicomachean Ethics*

Aristotle (384–322 B.C.*) was a more empirically minded philosopher than his teacher Plato. He has been regarded as the "greatest mind" of antiquity and, until the scientific revolution, the supreme intellectual authority in philosophy and the sciences. He contributed especially to physics, metaphysics, logic, and biology.*

Every craft and every investigation, and likewise every action and decision, seems to aim at some good; hence the good has been well described as that at which everything aims.

However, there is an apparent difference among the ends aimed at. For the end is sometimes an activity, sometimes a product beyond the activity; and where there is an end beyond the action, the product is by nature better than the activity.

Since there are many actions, crafts and sciences, the ends turn out to be many as well; for health is the end of medicine, a boat of boatbuilding, victory of generalship, and wealth of household management.

But whenever any of these sciences are subordinate to some one capacity—as e.g. bridlemaking and every other science producing equipment for horses are subordinate to horsemanship, while this and every action in warfare are in turn subordinate to generalship, and in the same way other sciences are subordinate to further ones—in each of these the end of the ruling science is more choiceworthy than all the ends subordinate to it, since it is the end for which those ends are also pursued. And here it does not matter whether the ends of the actions are the activities themselves, or some product beyond them, as in the sciences we have mentioned.

Aristotle, from *Nicomachean Ethics*, transl. by Terence Irwin, Hackett Publishing Company, Inc., copyright © 1985 by Terence Irwin.

Suppose, then, that (a) there is some end of the things we pursue in our actions which we wish for because of itself, and because of which we wish for the other things; and (b) we do not choose everything because of something else, since (c) if we do, it will go on without limit, making desire empty and futile; then clearly (d) this end will be the good, i.e. the best good.

Then surely knowledge of this good is also of great importance for the conduct of our lives, and if, like archers, we have a target to aim at, we are more likely to hit the right mark. If so, we should try to grasp, in outline at any rate, what the good is, and which science or capacity is concerned with it.

It seems to concern the most controlling science, the one that, more than any other, is the ruling science. And political science apparently has this character.

(1) For it is the one that prescribes which of the sciences ought to be studied in cities, and which ones each class in the city should learn, and how far.

(2) Again, we see that even the most honoured capacities, e.g. generalship, household management and rhetoric, are subordinate to it.

(3) Further, it uses the other sciences concerned with action, and moreover legislates what must be done and what avoided.

Hence its end will include the ends of the other sciences, and so will be the human good.

[This is properly called political science;] for though admittedly the good is the same for a city as for an individual, still the good of the city is apparently a greater and more complete good to acquire and preserve. For while it is satisfactory to acquire and preserve the good even for an individual, it is finer and more divine to acquire and preserve it for a people and for cities. And so, since our investigation aims at these [goods, for an individual and for a city], it is a sort of political science.

But let us return once again to the good we are looking for, and consider just what it could be, since it is apparently one thing in one action or craft, and another thing in another; for it is one thing in medicine, another in generalship, and so on for the rest.

What, then, is the good in each of these cases? Surely it is that for the sake of which the other things are done; and in medicine this is health, in generalship victory, in housebuilding a house, in another case something else, but in every action and decision it is the end, since it is for the sake of the end that everyone does the other things.

And so, if there is some end of everything that is pursued in action, this will be the good pursued in action; and if there are more ends than one, these will be the goods pursued in action.

Our argument has progressed, then, to the same conclusion [as before, that the highest end is the good]; but we must try to clarify this still more.

Though apparently there are many ends, we choose some of them, e.g. wealth, flutes and, in general, instruments, because of something else; hence it is clear that not all ends are complete. But the best good is apparently something complete. Hence, if only one end is complete, this will be what we are looking for; and if more than one are complete, the most complete of these will be what we are looking for.

An end pursued in itself, we say, is more complete than an end pursued because of something else; and an end that is never choice-worthy because of something else is more complete than ends that are choiceworthy both in themselves and because of this end; and hence an end that is always [choiceworthy, and also] choiceworthy in itself, never because of something else, is unconditionally complete.

Now happiness more than anything else seems unconditionally complete, since we always [choose it, and also] choose it because of itself, never because of something else.

Honour, pleasure, understanding and every virtue we certainly choose because of themselves, since we would choose each of them even if it had no further result, but we also choose them for the sake of happiness, supposing that through them we shall be happy. Happiness, by contrast, no one ever chooses for their sake, or for the sake of anything else at all.

The same conclusion [that happiness is complete] also appears to follow from self-sufficiency, since the complete good seems to be self-sufficient.

Now what we count as self-sufficient is not what suffices for a solitary person by himself, living an isolated life, but what suffices also for parents, children, wife and in general for friends and fellow-citizens, since a human being is a naturally political [animal]. Here, however, we must impose some limit; for if we extend the good to parents' parents and children's children and to friends of friends, we shall go on without limit; but we must examine this another time.

Anyhow, we regard something as self-sufficient when all by itself it makes a life choiceworthy and lacking nothing; and that is what we think happiness does.

Moreover, we think happiness is most choiceworthy of all goods, since it is not counted as one good among many. If it were counted as one among many, then, clearly, we think that the addition of the smallest of goods would make it more choiceworthy; for [the smallest good] that is added becomes an extra quantity of goods [so creating a good larger than the original good], and the larger of two goods is always more choiceworthy. [But we do not think any addition can make happiness more choiceworthy; hence it is most choiceworthy.]

Happiness, then, is apparently something complete and self-sufficient, since it is the end of the things pursued in action.

But presumably the remark that the best good is happiness is apparently something [generally] agreed, and what we miss is a clearer statement of what the best good is.

Well, perhaps we shall find the best good if we first find the function of a human being. For just as the good, i.e. [doing] well, for a flautist, a sculptor, and every craftsman, and, in general, for whatever has a function and [characteristic] action, seems to depend on its function, the same seems to be true for a human being, if a human being has some function.

Then do the carpenter and the leatherworker have their functions and actions, while a human being has none, and is by nature idle, without any function? Or, just as eye, hand, foot and, in general, every [bodily] part apparently has its functions, may we likewise ascribe to a human being some function besides all of theirs?

What, then, could this be? For living is apparently shared with plants, but what we are looking for is the special function of a human being; hence we should set aside the life of nutrition and growth. The life next in order is some sort of life of sense-perception; but this too is apparently shared, with horse, ox and every animal. The remaining possibility, then, is some sort of life of action of the [part of the soul] that has reason.

Now this [part has two parts, which have reason in different ways], one as obeying the reason [in the other part], the other as itself having reason and thinking. [We intend both.] Moreover, life is also spoken of in two ways [as capacity and as activity], and we must take [a human being's special function to be] life as activity, since this seems to be called life to a fuller extent.

(a) We have found, then, that the human function is the soul's activity that expresses reason [as itself having reason] or requires reason [as obeying reason]. (b) Now the function of F, e.g. of a harpist, is the same in kind, so we say, as the function of an excellent F, e.g. an excellent harpist. (c) The same is true unconditionally in every case, when we add to the function the superior achievement that expresses the virtue; for a harpist's function, e.g. is to play the harp, and a good harpist's is to do it well. (d) Now we take the human function to be a certain kind of life, and take this life to be the soul's activity and actions that express reason. (e) [Hence by (c) and (d)] the excellent man's function is to do this finely and well. (f) Each function is completed well when its completion expresses the proper virtue. (g) Therefore [by (d), (e) and (f)] the human good turns out to be the soul's activity that expresses virtue.

And if there are more virtues than one, the good will express the best and most complete virtue. Moreover, it will be in a complete life. For one swallow does not make a spring, nor does one day; nor, similarly, does one day or a short time make us blessed and happy.

This, then, is a sketch of the good; for, presumably, the outline must come first, to be filled in later. If the sketch is good, then anyone, it seems, can advance and articulate it, and in such cases time is a good discoverer or [at least] a good co-worker. That is also how the crafts have improved, since anyone can add what is lacking [in the outline].

However, we must also remember our previous remarks, so that we do not look for the same degree of exactness in all areas, but the degree that fits the subject-matter in each area and is proper to the investigation. For the carpenter's and the geometer's inquiries about the right angle are different also; the carpenter's is confined to the right angle's use-fulness for his work, whereas the geometer's concerns what, or what sort of thing, the right angle is, since he studies the truth. We must do the same, then, in other areas too, [seeking the proper degree of exactness], so that digressions do not overwhelm our main task.

Nor should we make the same demand for an explanation in all cases. Rather, in some cases it is enough to prove that something is true without explaining why it is true. This is so, e.g. with origins, where the fact that something is true is the first principle, i.e. the origin.

Some origins are studied by means of induction, some by means of perception, some by means of some sort of habituation, and others by other means. In each case we should try to find them out by means suited to their nature, and work hard to define them well. For they have a great influence on what follows; for the origin seems to be more than half the whole, and makes evident the answer to many of our questions.

3

St. Augustine,
"I Saw Only Death,"
from the *Confessions*

St. Augustine (354–430), Bishop of Hippo, was the last of the great thinkers in the tradition of classical philosophy. At the same time he was the most important of the Church Fathers and his work is the foundation of medieval theology and Protestant thought alike. A gifted writer, Augustine has rarely been surpassed in the description of intense emotion, and the following description of grief is one of the best in world literature.

I

During the period in which I first began to teach in the town of my birth, I had found a very dear friend, who was pursuing similar studies. He was about my own age, and was now coming, as I was, to the very flowering-time of young manhood. He had indeed grown up with me as a child and we had gone to school together and played together. Neither in those earlier days nor indeed in the later time of which I now speak was he a friend in the truest meaning of friendship: for there is no true friendship unless You weld it between souls that cleave together through that charity which is shed in our hearts by the Holy Ghost who is given to us. Yet it had become a friendship very dear to us, made the warmer by the ardor of studies pursued together. I had turned him from the true faith—in which being little more than a boy he was not deeply grounded—towards those superstitious and soul-destroying errors that my mother bewailed in me. With me he went astray in error, and my soul could not be without him. But You are ever close upon the heels of those who flee from You, for You are at once God of Vengeance and Fount of Mercy, and You turn us to

Augustine, from *Confessions*, transl. by Frank Sheed, 1993, Hackett Publishing Company, Inc.

Yourself by ways most wonderful. You took this man from the life of earth when he had completed scarcely a year in a friendship that had grown sweeter to me than all the sweetness of the life I knew. What man could recount all Your praises for the things he has experienced in his own single person? What was it, O my God, that You accomplished then and how unsearchable is the abyss of Your judgments! For he was in a high fever and when he had for a long time lain unconscious in a deathly sweat so that his life was despaired of, he was baptized. Naturally he knew nothing of it, and I paid little heed, since I took for granted that his mind would retain what he had learned from me and not what was done upon his body while he was unconscious. But it turned out very differently. The fever left him and he recovered. As soon as I could speak to him—which was as soon as he could speak to me, for I had not left him and indeed we depended too much upon each other—I began to mock, assuming that he would join me in mocking, the baptism which he had received when he had neither sense nor feeling. For by now he had been told of it. But he looked at me as if I had been his deadly enemy, and in a burst of independence that startled me warned me that if I wished to continue his friend I must cease that kind of talk. I was stupefied and deeply perturbed. I postponed telling him of my feelings until he should be well again, and thus in such condition of health and strength that I could discuss what was in my mind. But he was snatched from the reach of my folly that he might be safe with You for my future consolation. Within a few days he relapsed into his fever and died. And I was not there.

My heart was black with grief. Whatever I looked upon had the air of death. My native place was a prison-house and my home a strange unhappiness. The things we had done together became sheer torment without him. My eyes were restless looking for him, but he was not there. I hated all places because he was not in them. They could not say "He will come soon," as they would in his life when he was absent. I became a great enigma to myself and I was forever asking my soul why it was sad and why it disquieted me so sorely. And my soul knew not what to answer me. If I said "Trust in God" my soul did not obey—naturally, because the man whom she had loved and lost was nobler and more real than the imagined deity in whom I was bidding her trust. I had no delight but in tears, for tears had taken the place my friend had held in the love of my heart.

II

But now, Lord, all that has passed and time has dulled the ache of the wound. May I learn from You who are Truth, may I make the ear of my heart attentive to the word of Your mouth, that You may tell me why tears are so sweet to the sorrowful. Have You, for all that You are everywhere, cast our misery from You? You abide in Yourself, we are tossed from trial to trial: yet if we might not utter our sorrow to Your ears, nothing should remain for our hope. How does it come then that from the bitterness of life we can pluck fruit so sweet as is in mourning and weeping and sighing and the utterance of our woe? Are all these things such relief to our misery because of our hope that You hear them? Obviously this is so of our prayers, because they are uttered with the sole aim of reaching You. But is it so also of the sorrow and grief for a thing lost, in which I was then overwhelmed? I had no hope of bringing him back to life, nor for all my tears did I ask for this: simply I grieved and wept. For I was in misery and had lost my joy. Or is weeping really a bitter thing, pleasing to us only from a distaste for the things we once enjoyed and only while the distaste remains keen?

III

But why do I speak of these things? I should not be asking questions but making my confession to You. I was wretched, and every soul is wretched that is bound in affection of mortal things: it is tormented to lose them, and in their loss becomes aware of the wretchedness which in reality it had even before it lost them. Such was I at that time. And I wept most bitterly and in that bitterness found my only repose. I was wretched, yet I held my wretched life dearer than the friend for whose loss I was wretched. For although I would have liked to change the unhappiness of my life, yet I was more unwilling to lose my life itself than I had been to lose my friend; and I doubt if I would have been willing to lose it even to be with him—as the tradition is, whether true or false, of Orestes and Pylades, who wanted to die for each other and both together, because for either life without the other was worse than death. But in me there was an odd kind of feeling, the exact opposite of theirs, for I was at once utterly weary of life and in great fear of death. It may be that the more I loved him the more I hated and feared, as the cruellest enemy, that death which had taken him from me; and I was filled with the thought that it might snatch away any man as suddenly as it had snatched him. That this was then my mind, I still remember. Behold my heart, O my God, look deep within it; see how I remember, O my Hope, You who cleanse me from all the uncleanness of such affections *directing my eyes towards You and plucking my feet out of the snare.* I wondered that other mortals should live when he was dead whom I had loved as if he would never die; and I marvelled still more that he should be dead and I his other self living still. Rightly has a friend been called "the half of my soul." For I thought of my soul and his soul as one soul in two bodies; and my life was a horror to me because I would not live halved. And it may be that I feared to die lest thereby he should die wholly whom I had loved so deeply.

IV

O madness that knows not how to love men as men! O foolish man to bear the lot of man so rebelliously! I had both the madness and the folly. I raged and sighed and wept and was in torment, unable to rest, unable to think. I bore my soul all broken and bleeding and loathing to be borne by me; and I could find nowhere to set it down to rest. Not in shady groves, nor in mirth and music, nor in perfumed gardens, nor in formal banquets, nor in the delights of bedroom and bed, not in books nor in poetry could it find peace. I hated all things, hated the very light itself; and all that was not he was painful and wearisome, save only my tears: for in them alone did I find a little peace. When my soul gave over weeping, it was still crushed under the great burden of a misery which only by You, Lord, could be lightened and lifted. This I knew; but I had neither the will nor the strength—and what made it more impossible was that when I thought of You it was not as of something firm and solid. For my God was not yet You but the error and vain fantasy I held. When I tried to rest my burden upon that, it fell as through emptiness and was once more heavy upon me; and I remained to myself a place of unhappiness, in which I could not abide, yet from which I could not depart. For where was my heart to flee for refuge from my heart? Whither was I to fly from myself? To what place should I not follow myself? Yet leave my native place I did. For my eyes would look for him less where they had not been accustomed to see him. I left the town of Tagaste and came to Carthage.

V

Time takes no holiday. It does not roll idly by, but through our senses works its own wonders in the mind. Time came and went from one day to the next; in its coming and its passing it brought me other hopes and other memories, and little by little patched me up again with the kind of delights which had once been mine, and which in my grief I had abandoned. The place of that great grief was slowly taken, not perhaps by new griefs, but by the seeds from which new griefs should spring. For that first grief had pierced so easily and so deep only because I had spilt out my soul upon the sand, in loving a mortal man as if he were never to die. At any rate the comfort I found in other friends—and the pleasure I had with them in things of earth— did much to repair and remake me. And it was all one huge fable, one long lie; and by its adulterous caressing, my soul, which lay itching in my ears, was utterly corrupted. For my folly did not die whenever one of my friends died.

All kinds of things rejoiced my soul in their company—to talk and laugh and do each other kindnesses; read pleasant books together, pass from lightest jesting to talk of the deepest things and back again; differ without rancour, as a man might differ with himself, and when most rarely dissension arose find our normal agreement all the sweeter for it; teach each other or learn from each other; be impatient for the return of the absent, and welcome them with joy on their home-coming; these and such like things, proceeding from our hearts as we gave affection and received it back, and shown by face, by voice, by the eyes, and a thousand other pleasing ways, kindled a flame which fused our very souls and of many made us one.

VI

This is what men value in friends, and value so much that their conscience judges them guilty if they do not meet friendship with friendship, expecting nothing from their friend save such evidences of his affection. This is the root of our grief when a friend dies, and the blackness of our sorrow, and the steeping of the heart in tears for the joy that has turned to bitterness, and the feeling as though we were dead because he is dead. Blessed is the man that loves Thee, O God, and his friend in Thee, and his enemy for Thee. For he alone loses no one that is dear to him, if all are dear in God, who is never lost. And who is that God but our God, the God who made heaven and earth, who fills them because it is by filling them with Himself that he has made them? No man loses Thee, unless he goes from Thee; and in going from Thee, where does he go or where does he flee save from Thee to Thee—from God well-pleased to God angered? For where shall he not find Thy law fulfilled in his punishment? Thy law is truth and truth is Thou.

VII

Convert us, O God of hosts, and show us Thy face, and we shall be saved. Wherever the soul of man turns, unless towards God, it cleaves to sorrow, even though the things outside God and outside itself to which it cleaves may be things of beauty. For these lovely things would be nothing at all unless they were from Him. They rise and set: in their rising they begin to be, and they grow towards perfection, and once come to perfection they grow old, and they die: not all grow old but all die. Therefore when they rise and tend toward being, the more haste they make toward fullness of being, the more haste they make towards ceasing to be. That is their law. You have given them to be parts of a whole: they are not all existent at once, but in their departures and successions constitute the whole of which they are parts. Our own speech, which we utter by making sounds signifying meanings, follows the same principles. For there never could be a whole sentence unless one word ceased to be when its syllables had sounded and another took its place. In all such things let my soul praise You, O God, Creator of all things, but let it not cleave too close in love to them through the senses of the body. For they go their way and are no more; and they rend the soul with desires that can destroy it, for it longs to be one with the things it loves and to repose in them. But in them is no place of repose, because they do not abide. They pass, and who can follow them with any bodily sense? Or who can grasp them firm even while they are still here?

Our fleshly sense is slow because it is fleshly sense: and that is the limit of its being. It can do what it was made to do; but it has no power to hold things transient as they run their course from their due beginning to their due end. For in Your word, by which they are created, they hear their law: "From this point: not beyond that."

VIII

Be not foolish, my soul, nor let the ear of your heart be deafened with the clamor of your folly. Listen. The Word Himself calls to you to return, and with Him is the place of peace that shall not be broken, where your love will not be forsaken unless it first forsake. Things pass that other things may come in their place and this material universe be established in all its parts. "But do I depart anywhere?" says the Word of God. Fix your dwelling in Him, commit to God whatsoever you have: for it is from God. O my soul, wearied at last with emptiness, commit to Truth's keeping whatever Truth has given you, and you shall not lose any; and what is decayed in you shall be made clean, and what is sick shall be made well, and what is transient shall be reshaped and made new and established in you in firmness; and they shall not set you down where they themselves go, but shall stand and abide and you with them, before God who stands and abides forever.

Why, O perverse soul of mine, will you go on following your flesh? Rather turn, and let it follow you. Whatever things you perceive by fleshly sense you perceive only in part, not knowing the whole of which those things are but parts and yet they delight you so much. For if fleshly sense had been capable of grasping the whole—and had not for your punishment received part only of the whole as its just limit— you would wish that whatever exists in the present might pass on, that the whole might be perceived by you for your delight. What we speak, you hear by a bodily sense: and certainly you do not wish the same syllable to go on sounding but to pass away that other syllables may come and you may hear the whole speech. It is always so with all things that go to make up one whole: all that goes to make up the whole does not exist at one moment. If all could be perceived in one act of perception, it would obviously give more delight than any of the individual parts. But far better than all is He who made all; and He is our God. He does not pass away and there is none to take His place.

IX

If material things please you then praise God for them, but turn back your love upon Him who made them: lest in the things that please you, you displease Him. If souls please you, then love them in God because they are mutable in themselves but in Him firmly established: without Him they would pass and perish. Love them, I say, in Him, and draw as many souls with you to Him as you can, saying to them: "Him let us love: He made this world and is not far from it." For He did not simply make it and leave it: but as it is from Him so it is in Him. See where He is, wherever there is a savour of truth: He is in the most secret place of the heart, yet the heart has strayed from Him. O sinners, return to your own heart and abide in Him that made you. Stand with Him and you shall stand, rest in Him and you shall be at peace. Where are you going, to what bleak places? Where are you going? The good that you love is from Him: and insofar as it is likewise *for* Him it is good and lovely; but it will rightly be turned into bitterness, if it is unrightly loved and He deserted by whom it is. What goal are you making for, wandering around and about by ways so hard and laborious? Rest is not where you seek it. Seek what you seek, but it is not where you seek it. You seek happiness of life in the land of death, and it is not there. For how shall there be happiness of life where there is no life?

But our Life came down to this our earth and took away our death, slew death with the abundance of His own life: and He thundered, calling to us to return to Him into that secret place from which He came forth to us—coming first into the Virgin's womb, where humanity was wedded to Him, our mortal flesh, though not always to be mortal; and thence *like a bridegroom coming out of his bride chamber, rejoicing as a giant to run his course.* For He did not delay but rushed on, calling to us by what He said and what He did, calling to us by His death, life, descent, and ascension to return to Him. And He withdrew from our eyes, that we might return to our own heart and find Him. For He went away and behold He is still here. He would not be with us long, yet He did not leave us. He went back to that place which He had never left, for the world was made by Him. And He was in this world, and He came into this world to save sinners. Unto Him my soul confesses and He hears it, for it has sinned against Him. O ye sons of men, how long will ye be so slow of heart? Even now when Life has come down to you, will you not ascend and live? But to what high place shall you climb, since you are in a high place and have *set your mouth against the heavens?* First descend that you may ascend, ascend to God. For in mounting up *against* God you fell. Tell the souls of men to weep in this valley of tears, and so bear them up with you to God, because it is by His Spirit that you are speaking this to them, if in your speaking you are on fire with the fire of charity.

4

Dionysius the Areopagite,
"On Life,"
from *The Divine Names*

Dionysius the Areopagite, who lived in the first century A.D., *was converted to Christianity by St. Paul in Athens, according to Acts 17:34. "A few men became followers of Paul and believed. Among them was Dionysius. . . . "* *The writings attributed to him were probably written down by "Pseudo-Dionysius," in the sixth century* A.D., *and became important in subsequent Christian theology.* *They include* The Divine Names, On Mystical Theology, *and* On the Celestial Hierarchy.

Now let us praise the Eternal Life from which comes Life itself and all life, and from which is imparted to all things, howsoever they participate in life, the life appropriate to each.

Now the life of the immortal angels and their immortality, their indestructible nature, their angelic perpetual motion, are and subsist from It and for Its sake. Wherefore they are called ever-living and immortal, and yet not immortal, because they have not from themselves their immortal being and eternal life, but they proceed from the life-giving Cause which creates and sustains all life. And just as we spoke of Him who is as the essential eternity of being itself, so do we now say that the Divine Life above all life is Life itself and is the life-giver and sustainer of all life. And all life and vital movement come from that Life which is above all life. From It souls have their immortality and all animals and plants have their life as a distant echo of that Life. And when this is taken away, all life fails, as the Scripture says, and even those who have failed, through their incapacity to participate in Its immortality, receive life once more when they turn again to It.

And It gives first to the self-subsistent life its essential life, and to the whole of life and to each living being It gives that which is adapted

Dionysius the Areopagite, *The Divine Names*, The Shrine of Wisdom, Fintry, England: 1957.

to its own nature: to the supercelestial lives the immaterial and the Godlike, a changeless immortality, and their unswerving and inerrant perpetual motion, while Its boundless outflowing through Its all-prolific Goodness extends even to the life of daimones. For daimones have not their existence and life and perpetuation from any other cause than this. Moreover It imparts to men such a measure of angelic life as their composite nature can receive, and through Its overflowing love for man It turns and calls us, when we have strayed from It, back to Itself and, more divinely still, It has promised to transform us wholly— our souls and the bodies joined to them—to a perfect life and immortality: a fact which perhaps to the ancients seemed unnatural, but to me and to thee and to the truth seems Divine and above nature—that is to say, above our visible nature, not above that omnipotent Nature of Divine Life. For to this Life, being the nature of all living things, and especially the more divine of these, no life is unnatural or supernatural.

Therefore the foolish and controversial words of Simon* must be banished from the company of the godly and from thy holy soul. For while thinking himself wise, he overlooked, I think, the truth that no man of balanced mind should use the order of that which is evident to the senses as a means for attacking the invisible Cause of all. And we must answer him that it is his statement that is against nature, since nothing is contrary to the Cause of all.

From this eternal Life all animals and plants are filled with life and energy; and whether you speak of life as intellectual, or rational, or sensitive, or vegetative life, or merely increment, or whatever kind of life, or principle of life, or essence of life it may be, it has its being from This which is above every life; and from It both lives and imparts life; and in It pre-subsists unitedly as in its Cause. For the super-vital Life and life-giving Source of Life is the cause of all life, the producer of life, the fulfiller of life, and the differentiator of life. And the attributes of every kind of life must be predicated of It in accordance with Its prolific generation of life and the multiform variety under which It is seen and acclaimed in all life, and because It is in need of nothing, but is rather the Super-plenitude of Life, Super-vital, or whatever other name can be humanly applied to the Ineffable Life.

---

* Simon denied the resurrection of the body.

5

St. Thomas Aquinas, "That All Things Are Directed to One End, Which Is God," from the *Summa contra Gentiles*

St. Thomas Aquinas (1225–1274), the author of the Summa Theologica, *was the foremost of the medieval philosophers and theologians. He has been since 1879 the official philosopher of the Roman Catholic Church.*

That All Things Are Directed to One End, Which Is God

From the foregoing it is clear that all things are directed to one good as their last end.

For if nothing tends to something as its end, except in so far as this is good, it follows that good, as such, is an end. Consequently that which is the supreme good is supremely the end of all. Now there is but one supreme good, namely God, as we have shown in the First Book.[1] Therefore all things are directed to the highest good, namely God, as their end.

Again. *That which is supreme in any genus is the cause of everything in that genus.*[2] Thus fire which is supremely hot is the cause of heat in other bodies. Therefore the supreme good, namely God, is the cause of goodness in all things good. Therefore He is the cause of every end being an end, since whatever is an end is such in so far as it is good. Now *the cause that a thing is so is itself more so.*[3] Therefore God is supremely the end of all things.

Further. In every genus of causes, the first cause is more a cause

St. Thomas Aquinas, *Summa Contra Gentiles,* Book III, "The End of Man," in *Basic Writings of St. Thomas Aquinas,* ed. Anton C. Pegis, Random House, New York, 1945.

1. *C. G.,* I, 42.
2. Aristotle, *Metaph.,* I a, 1 (993b 22).
3. Aristotle, *Post. Anal.,* I, 2 (72a 28).

than the second cause, since the second cause is not a cause save through the first. Therefore that which is the first cause in the order of final causes must needs be more the final cause of each thing than the proximate final cause. Now God is the first cause in the order of final causes, for He is supreme in the order of good things. Therefore He is the end of each thing more even than any proximate end.

Moreover. In all ordered ends the last must needs be the end of each preceding end. Thus if a potion be mixed to be given to a sick man, and is given to him that he may be purged, and he be purged that he may be lowered, and lowered that he may be healed, it follows that health is the end of the lowering, and of the purging, and of those that precede. Now all things are ordered in various degrees of goodness to the one supreme good, which is the cause of all goodness; and so, since good has the nature of an end, all things are ordered under God as preceding ends under the last end. Therefore God must be the end of all.

Furthermore. The particular good is directed to the common good as its end, for the being of the part is for the sake of the being of the whole.[4] So it is that *the good of the nation is more godlike than the good of one man.*[5] Now the supreme good, namely God, is the common good, since the good of all things depends on Him; and the good, whereby each thing is good, is the particular good of that thing, and of those that depend thereon. Therefore all things are directed to one good, namely God, as their end.

Again. Order among ends is consequent on the order among agents. For just as the supreme agent moves all second agents, so all the ends of second agents must be directed to the end of the supreme agent, since whatever the supreme agent does, it does for its own end. Now the supreme agent is the active principle of the actions of all inferior agents, by moving all to their actions, and consequently to their ends. Hence it follows that all the ends of second agents are ordered by the first agent to its own end. Now the first agent in all things is God, as we proved in the Second Book.[6] And His will has no other end but His own goodness, which is Himself, as we showed in the First Book.[7]

4. Aristotle, *Polit.*, I, 4 (1254a 9).
5. Aristotle, *Eth.*, I, 2 (1094b 9) [p. 17 of this volume. Eds.].
6. *C. G.*, II, 15.
7. *C. G.*, I, 74.

Therefore all things, whether they were made by Him immediately, or by means of secondary causes, are ordered to God as their end. But this applies to all things, for, as we proved in the Second Book,[8] there can be nothing that has not its being from Him. Therefore all things are ordered to God as their end.

Moreover. The last end of every maker, as such, is himself, for what we make we use for our own sake; and if at any time a man make a thing for the sake of something else, it is referred to his own good, whether his use, his pleasure, or his virtue. Now God is the producing cause of all things: of some immediately, of others by means of other causes, as we have explained above.[9] Therefore He is the end of all things.

And again. The end holds the primary place among causes, and it is from it that all other causes derive their actual causality; since the agent does not act except for the end, as was proved.[10] Now it is due to the agent that the matter is brought to the actuality of the form, and therefore the matter is made actually the matter, and the form is made the form, of this particular thing, through the agent's action, and consequently through the end. The later end also is the cause that the preceding end is intended as an end; for a thing is not moved towards a proximate end except for the sake of the last end. Therefore the last end is the first cause of all. Now it must necessarily befit the First Being, namely God, to be the first cause of all, as we proved above.[11] Therefore God is the last end of all.

Hence it is written (*Prov.* xvi. 4): *The Lord hath made all things for himself;* and (*Apoc.* xxii. 13), *I am Alpha and Omega, the first and the last.*

How God Is the End of Things

It remains to ask how God is the end of all things. This will be made clear from what has been said.

For He is the end of all things, yet so as to precede all in being.[12]

8. *C. G.,* II, 15.
9. Ibid.
10. Ch. 2 [not included in this volume. Eds.].
11. *C. G.,* II, 15.
12. *C. G.,* I, 13.

Now there is an end which, though it holds the first place in causing in so far as it is in the intention, is nevertheless last in execution. This applies to any end which the agent establishes by his action. Thus the physician by his action establishes health in the sick man, which is nevertheless his end. There is also an end which, just as it precedes in causing, so also does it precede in being. Thus, that which one intends to acquire by one's motion or action is said to be one's end. For instance, fire seeks to reach a higher place by its movement, and the king seeks to take a city by fighting. Accordingly, God is the end of things as something to be obtained by each thing in its own way.

Again. God is at once the last end of things and the first agent, as we have shown.[13] Now the end effected by the agent's action cannot be the first agent, but rather is it the agent's effect. God, therefore, cannot be the end of things as though He were something effected, but only as something already existing and to be acquired.

Further. If a thing act for the sake of something already in existence, and if by its action some result ensue, then something through the agent's action must accrue to the thing for the sake of which it acts; and thus soldiers fight for the cause of their captain, to whom victory accrues, which the soldiers bring about by their actions. Now nothing can accrue to God from the action of anything whatever, since His goodness is perfect in every way, as we proved in the First Book.[14] It follows, then, that God is the end of things, not as something made or effected by them, nor as though He obtained something from things, but in this way alone, that He is obtained by them.

Moreover. The effect must tend to the end in the same way as the agent acts for the end. Now God, who is the first agent of all things, does not act as though He gained something by His action, but as bestowing something thereby; since He is not in potentiality so that He can acquire something, but solely in perfect actuality, whereby He is able to bestow. Things therefore are not ordered to God as to an end to which something will be added; they are ordered to Him to obtain God Himself from Him according to their measure, since He is their end.

13. ["That All Things Are Directed . . ." Eds.]
14. *C. G.*, I. 37ff.

That All Things Tend to be Like unto God

From the fact that they acquire the divine goodness, creatures are made like unto God. Therefore, if all things tend to God as their last end, so as to acquire His goodness,[15] it follows that the last end of things is to become like unto God.

Moreover. The agent is said to be the end of the effect in so far as the effect tends to be like the agent; and hence it is that *the form of the generator is the end of the act of generation.*[16] Now God is the end of things in such wise as to be also their first producing cause. Therefore all things tend to a likeness to God, as their last end.

Again. Things give evidence that *they naturally desire to be,*[17] so that if any are corruptible, they naturally resist corruptives, and tend to where they can be safeguarded, as the fire tends upwards and earth downwards. Now all things have being in so far as they are like God, Who is self-subsistent being, since they are all beings only by participation. Therefore all things desire as their last end to be like God.

Further. All creatures are images of the first agent, namely God, since *the agent produces its like.*[18] Now the perfection of an image consists in representing the original by a likeness to it, for this is why an image is made. Therefore all things exist for the purpose of acquiring a likeness to God, as for their last end.

Again. Each thing by its movement or action tends to some good as its end, as was proved above.[19] Now a thing partakes of good in so far as it is like to the first goodness, which is God. Therefore all things, by their movements and actions, tend to a likeness to God as to their last end.

That to Know God Is the End of Every Intellectual Substance

Now, seeing that all creatures, even those that are devoid of reason, are directed to God as their last end, and that all reach this end in so far as they have some share of a likeness to Him, the intellectual creature attains to Him in a special way, namely, through its proper

15. Ch. 18. ["How God Is the End of Things" Eds.].
16. Aristotle, *Phys.*, II, 7 (198a 26).
17. Aristotle, *Eth.*, IX, 7 (1168a 5); 9 (1170a 26).
18. Aristotle, *De Gener.*, I, 7 (324a II).
19. Ch. 16 [not included in this volume. Eds.].

operation, by understanding Him. Consequently this must be the end of the intellectual creature, namely, to understand God.

For, as we have shown above,[20] God is the end of each thing, and hence, as far as it is possible to it, each thing intends to be united to God as its last end. Now a thing is more closely united to God by reaching in a way to the very substance of God; which happens when it knows something of the divine substance, rather than when it reaches to a divine likeness. Therefore the intellectual substance tends to the knowledge of God as its last end.

Again. The operation proper to a thing is its end, for it is its second perfection; so that when a thing is well conditioned for its proper operation it is said to be fit and good. Now understanding is the proper operation of the intellectual substance, and consequently is its end. Therefore, whatever is most perfect in this operation is its last end; and especially in those operations which are not directed to some product, such as understanding and sensation. And since operations of this kind take their species from their objects, by which also they are known, it follows that the more perfect the object of any such operation, the more perfect is the operation. Consequently to understand the most perfect intelligible, namely God, is the most perfect in the genus of the operation which consists in understanding. Therefore to know God by an act of understanding is the last end of every intellectual substance.

Someone, however, might say that the last end of an intellectual substance consists indeed in understanding the best intelligible object, but that what is the best intelligible for this or that intellectual substance is not absolutely the best intelligible; and that the higher the intellectual substance, the higher is its best intelligible. So that possibly the supreme intellectual substance has for its best intelligible object that which is best absolutely, and its happiness will consist in understanding God; whereas the happiness of any lower intellectual substance will consist in understanding some lower intelligible object, which however will be the highest thing understood by that substance. Especially would it seem not to be in the power of the human intellect to understand that which is absolutely the best intelligible, because of its weakness; for it is as much adapted for knowing the supreme intelligible *as the owl's eye for seeing the sun.*[21]

20. ["That All Things Are Directed . . ." Eds.]
21. Aristotle, *Metaph.,* I a, 1 (993b 9).

Nevertheless it is evident that the end of any intellectual substance, even the lowest, is to understand God. For it has been shown above that God is the last end towards which all things tend.[22] And the human intellect, although the lowest in the order of intelligent substances, is superior to all that are devoid of understanding. Since then a more noble substance has not a less noble end, God will be the end also of the human intellect. Now every intelligent being attains to its last end by understanding it, as we have proved. Therefore the human intellect attains to God as its end, by understanding Him.

Again. Just as things devoid of intellect tend to God as their end by way of assimilation, so do intellectual substances by way of knowledge, as clearly appears from what has been said. Now, although things devoid of reason tend towards a likeness to their proximate causes, the intention of nature does not rest there, but has for its end a likeness to the highest good, as we have proved,[23] although they are able to attain to this likeness in a most imperfect manner. Therefore, however, little be the knowledge of God to which the intellect is able to attain, this will be the intellect's last end, rather than a perfect knowledge of lower intelligibles.

Moreover. Everything desires most of all its last end. Now the human intellect desires, loves and enjoys the knowledge of divine things, although it can grasp but little about them, more than the perfect knowledge which it has of the lowest things. Therefore man's last end is to understand God in some way.

Further. Everything tends to a divine likeness as its own end. Therefore a thing's last end is that whereby it is most of all like God. Now the intellectual creature is especially likened to God in that it is intellectual, since this likeness belongs to it above other creatures, and includes all other likenesses. And in this particular kind of likeness it is more like God in understanding actually than in understanding habitually or potentially, because God is always actually understanding, as we proved in the First Book.[24] Furthermore, in understanding actually, the intellectual creature is especially like God in understanding God; for by understanding Himself God understand all other things,

22. ["That All Things Are Directed . . ." Eds.]
23. ["That All Things Tend to Be Like unto God" Eds.]
24. *C. G.*, I, 56.

as we proved in the First Book.[25] Therefore the last end of every intellectual substance is to understand God.

Again. That which is lovable only because of another is for the sake of that which is lovable for its own sake alone; because we cannot go on indefinitely in the appetite of nature, since then nature's desire would be in vain, for it is impossible to pass through an infinite number of things. Now all practical sciences, arts and powers are lovable only for the sake of something else, since their end is not knowledge, but work. But speculative sciences are lovable for their own sake, for their end is knowledge itself. Nor can we find any action in human life that is not directed to some other end, with the exception of speculative consideration. For even playful actions, which seem to be done without any purpose, have some end due to them, namely that the mind may be relaxed, and that thereby we may afterwards become more fit for studious occupations; or otherwise we should always have to be playing, if play were desirable for its own sake, and this is unreasonable. Accordingly, the practical arts are directed to the speculative arts, and again every human operation, to intellectual speculation, as its end. Now, in all sciences and arts that are mutually ordered, the last end seems to belong to the one from which others take their rules and principles. Thus the art of sailing, to which belongs the ship's purpose, namely its use, provides rules and principles to the art of ship-building. And such is the relation of first philosophy to other speculative sciences, for all others depend thereon, since they derive their principles from it, and are directed by it in defending those principles; and moreover first philosophy is wholly directed to the knowledge of God as its last end, and is consequently called the *divine science*.[26] Therefore the knowledge of God is the last end of all human knowledge and activity.

Furthermore. In all mutually ordered agents and movers, the end of the first agent and mover must be the end of all, even as the end of the commander-in-chief is the end of all who are soldiering under him. Now of all the parts of man, the intellect is the highest mover, for it moves the appetite, by proposing its object to it; and the intellective appetite, or will, moves the sensitive appetites, namely the irascible and concupiscible. Hence it is that we do not obey the concupiscence, unless the will command; while the sensitive appetite, when the will

25. *C. G.*, I, 49.
26. Aristotle, *Metaph.*, I, 2 (983a 6).

has given its consent, moves the body. Therefore the end of the intellect is the end of all human actions. *Now the intellect's end and good are the true,*[27] and its last end is the first truth. Therefore the last end of the whole man, and of all his deeds and desires, is to know the first truth, namely, God.

Moreover. Man has a natural desire to know the causes of whatever he sees; and so through wondering at what they saw, and not knowing its cause, men first began to philosophize, and when they had discovered the cause they were at rest. Nor do they cease inquiring until they come to the first cause; and *then do we deem ourselves to know perfectly when we know the first cause.*[28] Therefore man naturally desires, as his last end, to know the first cause. But God is the first cause of all things. Therefore man's last end is to know God.

Besides. Man naturally desires to know the cause of any known effect. But the human intellect knows universal being. Therefore it naturally desires to know its cause, which is God alone, as we proved in the Second Book.[29] Now one has not attained to one's last end until the natural desire is at rest. Therefore the knowledge of any intelligible object is not enough for man's happiness, which is his last end, unless he know God also, which knowledge terminates his natural desire as his last end. Therefore this very knowledge of God is man's last end.

Further. A body that tends by its natural appetite to its place is moved all the more vehemently and rapidly the nearer it approaches its end. Hence Aristotle proves that a natural straight movement cannot be towards an indefinite point, because it would not be more moved afterwards than before.[30] Hence that which tends more vehemently to a thing afterwards than before is not moved towards an indefinite point but towards something fixed. Now this we find in the desire of knowledge, for the more one knows, the greater one's desire to know. Consequently, man's natural desire in knowledge tends to a definite end. This can be none other than the highest thing knowable, which is God. Therefore the knowledge of God is man's last end.

Now the last end of man and of any intelligent substance is called *happiness or beatitude,* for it is this that every intellectual substance

27. Aristotle, *Eth.,* VI, 2 (1139a 27).
28. Aristotle, *Metaph.,* I, 3 (983a 25).
29. *C. G.,* II, 15.
30. *De Caelo,* I, 8 (277a 18).

desires as its last end, and for its own sake alone. Therefore the last beatitude or happiness of any intellectual substance is to know God. Hence it is said (*Matt.* v. 8): *Blessed are the clean of heart, for they shall see God;* and (*Jo.* xvii. 3): *This is eternal life, that they may know thee, the only true God.* Aristotle himself agrees with this judgment when he says that man's ultimate happiness is *speculative, and this with regard to the highest object of speculation.*[31]

Does Happiness Consist in an Act of the Will?

Since the intellectual substance attains to God by its operation, not only by an act of understanding but also by an act of the will, through desiring and loving Him, and through delighting in Him, someone might think that man's last end and ultimate happiness consists, not in knowing God, but in loving Him, or in some other act of the will towards Him; [1] especially since the object of the will is the good, which has the nature of an end, whereas the true, which is the object of the intellect, has not the nature of an end except in so far as it also is a good. Therefore, seemingly, man does not attain to his last end by an act of his intellect, but rather by an act of his will.

[2] Further. The ultimate perfection of operation is delight, *which perfects operation as beauty perfects youth,* as the Philosopher says.[32] Hence, if the last end be a perfect operation, it would seem that it must consist in an act of the will rather than of the intellect.

[3] Again. Delight apparently is desired for its own sake, so that it is never desired for the sake of something else; for it is silly to ask of anyone why he seeks to be delighted. Now this is a condition of the ultimate end, namely, that it be sought for its own sake. Therefore, seemingly, the last end consists in an act of the will rather than of the intellect.

[4] Moreover. All agree in their desire of the last end, for it is a natural desire. But more people seek delight than knowledge. Therefore delight would seem to be the last end rather than knowledge.

[5] Furthermore. The will is seemingly a higher power than the intellect, for the will moves the intellect to its act; since when a person wills, his intellect considers by an act what he holds by a habit. There-

31. *Eth.*, X, 7 (1177a 18).
32. *Eth.*, X, 4 (1174b 31).

fore, seemingly the action of the will is more noble than the action of the intellect. Therefore, it would seem that the last end, which is beatitude, consists in an act of the will rather than of the intellect.

But this can be clearly shown to be impossible.

For since happiness is the proper good of the intellectual nature, it must needs become the intellectual nature according to that which is proper thereto. Now appetite is not proper to the intellectual nature, but is in all things, although it is found diversely in diverse things. This diversity, however, arises from the fact that things are diversely related to knowledge. For things wholly devoid of knowledge have only a natural appetite; those that have a sensitive knowledge have also a sensitive appetite, under which the irascible and concupiscible appetites are comprised; and those which have intellectual knowledge have also an appetite proportionate to that knowledge, namely, the will. The will, therefore, in so far as it is an appetite, is not proper to the intellectual nature, but only in so far as it is dependent on the intellect. On the other hand, the intellect is in itself proper to the intellectual nature. Therefore, beatitude or happiness consists principally and essentially in an act of the intellect, rather than in an act of the will.

Again. In all powers that are moved by their objects, the object is naturally prior to the acts of those powers, even as the mover is naturally prior to the movable being moved. Now the will is such a power, for the appetible object moves the appetite. Therefore the will's object is naturally prior to its act, and consequently its first object precedes its every act. Therefore an act of the will cannot be the first thing willed. But this is the last end, which is beatitude. Therefore beatitude or happiness cannot be the very act of the will.

Besides. In all those powers which are able to reflect on their acts, their act must first bear on some other object, and afterwards the power is brought to bear on its own act. For if the intellect understands that it understands, we must suppose first that it understands some particular thing, and that afterwards it understands that it understands; for this very act of understanding, which the intellect understands, must have an object. Hence either we must go on forever, or if we come to some first thing understood, this will not be an act of understanding, but some intelligible thing. In the same way, the first thing willed cannot be the very act of willing, but must be some other good. Now the first thing willed by an intellectual nature is beatitude or happiness; because it is for its sake that we will whatever we will. Therefore happiness cannot consist in an act of the will.

Further. The truth of a thing's nature is derived from those things which constitute its substance; for a true man differs from a man in a picture by the things which constitute man's substance. Now false happiness does not differ from true in an act of the will; because, whatever be proposed to the will as the supreme good, whether truly or falsely, it makes no difference to the will in its desiring, loving, or enjoying that good: the difference is on the part of the intellect, as to whether the good proposed as supreme be truly so or not. Therefore beatitude or happiness consists essentially in an act of the intellect rather than of the will.

Again. If an act of the will were happiness itself, this act would be an act either of desire, or love, or delight. But desire cannot possibly be the last end. For desire implies that the will is tending to what it has not yet; and this is contrary to the very notion of the last end.— Nor can love be the last end. For a good is loved not only while it is in our possession, but even when it is not, because it is through love that we seek by desire what we have not; and if the love of a thing we possess is more perfect, this arises from the fact that we possess the good we love. It is one thing, therefore, to possess the good which is our end, and another to love it; for love was imperfect before we possessed the end, and perfect after we obtained possession.—Nor again is delight the last end. For it is possession of the good that causes delight, whether we are conscious of possessing it actually, or call to mind our previous possession, or hope to possess it in the future. Therefore delight is not the last end.—Therefore no act of the will can be happiness itself essentially.

Furthermore. If delight were the last end, it would be desirable for its own sake. But this is not true. For the desirability of a delight depends on what gives rise to the delight, since that which arises from good and desirable operations is itself good and desirable, but that which arises from evil operations is itself evil and to be avoided. Therefore its goodness and desirability are from something else, and consequently it is not itself the last end or happiness.

Moreover. The right order of things agrees with the order of nature, for in the natural order things are ordered to their end without any error. Now, in the natural order delight is for the sake of operation, and not conversely. For it is to be observed that nature has joined delight with those animal operations which are clearly ordered to necessary ends: for instance, to the use of food that is ordered to the preservation of the individual, and to sexual matters, that are appointed for the preservation of the species; since were there no pleasure, animals would abstain from the use of these necessary things. Therefore delight cannot be the last end.

Again. Delight, seemingly, is nothing else than the quiescence of the will in some becoming good, just as desire is the inclining of the will towards the attaining of some good. Now just as by his will a man is inclined towards an end, and rests in it, so too natural bodies have a natural inclination to their respective ends, and are at rest when they have once attained their end. Now it is absurd to say that the end of the movement of a heavy body is not to be in its proper place, but that it is the quiescence of the inclination towards that place. For if it were nature's chief intent that this inclination should be quiescent, it would not give such an inclination; but it gives the inclination so that the body may tend towards its proper place, and when it has arrived there, as though it were its end, quiescence of the inclination follows. Hence this quiescence is not the end, but accompanies the end. Neither therefore is delight the ultimate end, but accompanies it. Much less therefore is happiness any act of the will.

Besides. If a thing have something extrinsic for its end, the operation whereby it first obtains that thing will be called its last end. Thus, for those whose end is money possession is said to be their end, but not love or desire. Now the last end of the intellectual substance is God. Hence that operation of man whereby he first obtains God is essentially his happiness or beatitude. And this is understanding, since we cannot will what we do not understand. Therefore man's ultimate happiness is essentially to know God by the intellect; it is not an act of the will.

From what has been said we can now solve the arguments that were objected in the contrary sense. For it does not necessarily follow that happiness is essentially the very act of the will, from the fact that it is the object of the will, through being the highest good, as the *first argument* reasoned. On the contrary, the fact that it is the first object of the will shows that it is not an act of the will, as appears from what we have said.

Nor does it follow that whatever perfects a thing in anyway whatever must be the end of that thing, as the *second objection* argued. For a thing perfects another in two ways: first, it perfects a thing that has its species; secondly, it perfects a thing that it may have its species. Thus the perfection of a house, considered as already having its species, is that to which the species "house" is directed, namely to be a dwelling;

for one would not build a house but for that purpose, and consequently we must include this in the definition of a house, if the definition is to be perfect. On the other hand, the perfection that conduces to the species of a house is both that which is directed to the completion of the species, for instance, its substantial principles; and also that which conduces to the preservation of the species, for instance, the buttresses which are made to support the building; as well as those things which make the house more fit for use, for instance, the beauty of the house. Accordingly, that which is the perfection of a thing, considered as already having its species, is its end; as the end of a house is to be a dwelling. Likewise, the operation proper to a thing, its use, as it were, is its end. On the other hand, whatever perfects a thing by conducing to its species is not the end of that thing; in fact, the thing itself is its end, for matter and form are for the sake of the species. For although the form is the end of generation, it is not the end of the thing already generated and having its species, but is required in order that the species be complete. Again, whatever preserves the thing in its species, such as health and the nutritive power, although it perfects the animal, is not the animal's end, but vice versa. And again, whatever adapts a thing for the perfection of its proper specific operations, and for the easier attainment of its proper end, is not the end of that thing, but vice versa; for instance, a man's comeliness and bodily strength, and the like, of which the Philosopher says that they *conduce to happiness instrumentally.*[33]—Now delight is a perfection of operation, not as though operation were directed thereto in respect of its species, for thus it is directed to other ends (thus, eating, in respect of its species, is directed to the preservation of the individual); but it is like a perfection that is conducive to a thing's species, since for the sake of the delight we perform more attentively and becomingly an operation we delight in. Hence the Philosopher says that *delight perfects operation as beauty perfects youth,*[34] for beauty is for the sake of the one who has youth and not *vice versa.*

Nor is the fact that men seek delight not for the sake of something else but for its own sake a sufficient indication that delight is the last end, as the *third objection* argued. Because delight, though it is not the last end, nevertheless accompanies the last end, since delight arises from the attainment of the end.

33. *Eth.,* I, 8 (1099b 2); 9 (1099b 28).
34. *Op. cit.,* X, 4 (1174b 31).

Nor do more people seek the pleasure that comes from knowledge than knowledge itself. But more there are who seek sensible delights than intellectual knowledge and the delight consequent thereto; because those things that are outside us are better known to the majority, in that human knowledge takes its beginning from sensible objects.

The suggestion put forward by the *fifth argument*, that the will is a higher power than the intellect, as being the latter's motive power, is clearly untrue. Because the intellect moves the will first and *per se*, for the will, as such, is moved by its object, which is the apprehended good; whereas the will moves the intellect accidentally as it were, in so far, namely, as the act of understanding is itself apprehended as a good, and on that account is desired by the will, with the result that the intellect understands actually. Even in this, the intellect precedes the will, for the will would never desire understanding, did not the intellect first apprehend its understanding as a good.—And again, the will moves the intellect to actual operation in the same way as an agent is said to move; whereas the intellect moves the will in the same way as the end moves, for the good understood is the end of the will. Now the agent is moving presupposes the end, for the agent does not move except for the sake of the end. It is therefore clear that the intellect is higher than the will absolutely, while the will is higher than intellect accidentally and in a restricted sense.

That Human Happiness Does Not Consist in Carnal Pleasures

From what has been said it is clearly impossible that human happiness consist in pleasures of the body, the chief of which are pleasures of the table and of sex.

It has been shown that according to nature's order pleasure is for the sake of operation, and not conversely.[35] Therefore, if an operation be not the ultimate end, the consequent pleasure can neither be the ultimate end, nor accompany the ultimate end. Now it is manifest that the operations which are followed by the pleasures mentioned above are not the last end; for they are directed to certain manifest ends: eating, for instance, to the preservation of the body, and carnal intercourse to the begetting of children. Therefore the aforesaid pleasures are not the last end, nor do they accompany the last end. Therefore happiness does not consist in them.

35. ["Does Happiness Consist of an Act of Will?" Eds.]

Again. The will is higher than the sensitive appetite, for it moves the sensitive appetite, as was stated above.[36] But happiness does not consist in an act of the will, as we have already proved.[37] Much less therefore does it consist in the aforesaid pleasures which are seated in the sensitive appetite.

Moreover. Happiness is a good proper to man, for it is an abuse of terms to speak of brute animals as being happy. Now these pleasures are common to man and brute. Therefore we must not assign happiness to them.

The last end is the most noble of things belonging to a reality, for it has the nature of that which is best. But the aforementioned pleasures do not befit man according to what is most noble in him, namely, the intellect, but according to the sense. Therefore happiness is not to be located in such pleasures.

Besides. The highest perfection of man cannot consist in his being united to things lower than himself, but consists in his being united to something above him; for the end is better than that which tends to the end. Now the above pleasures consist in man's being united through his senses to things beneath him, namely, certain sensible things. Therefore we must not assign happiness to such pleasures.

Further. That which is not good unless it be moderate is not good in itself, but receives its goodness from its moderator. Now the use of the aforesaid pleasures is not good for man unless it be moderate; for otherwise they would frustrate one another. Therefore these pleasures are not in themselves man's good. But the highest good is good of itself, because that which is good of itself is better than what is good through another. Therefore such pleasures are not man's highest good, which is happiness.

Again. In all *per se* predications, if A be predicated of B absolutely, an increase in A will be predicated of an increase in B. Thus if a hot thing heats, a hotter thing heats more, and the hottest thing will heat most. Accordingly, if the pleasures in question were good in themselves, it would follow that to use them very much would be very good. But this is clearly false, because it is considered sinful to use them too much; besides, it is hurtful to the body, and hinders pleasures of the same kind. Therefore they are not *per se* man's good, and human happiness does not consist in them.

36. *Ibid.*
37. *Ibid.*

Again. Acts of virtue are praiseworthy through being ordered to happiness.[38] If therefore human happiness consisted in the aforesaid pleasures, an act of virtue would be more praiseworthy in acceding to them than in abstaining from them. But this is clearly untrue, for the act of temperance is especially praised in abstinence from pleasures; whence that act takes its name. Therefore man's happiness is not in these pleasures.

Furthermore. The last end of everything is God, as was proved above.[39] We must therefore posit as man's last end that by which especially man approaches to God. Now man is hindered by the aforesaid pleasures from his chief approach to God, which is effected by contemplation to which these same pleasures are a very great hindrance, since more than anything they plunge man into the midst of sensible things, and consequently withdraw him from intelligible things. Therefore human happiness is not to be placed in bodily pleasures.

Hereby is refuted the error of the Epicureans who ascribed man's happiness to pleasures of this kind. In their person Solomon says (*Eccles.* v. 17): *This therefore hath seemed good to me, that a man should eat and drink, and enjoy the fruit of his labor . . . and this is his portion;* and (*Wis.* ii. 9): *Let us everywhere leave tokens of joy, for this is our portion, and this is our lot.*

The error of the Cerinthians is also refuted. For they *pretended that, in the state of final happiness, after the resurrection Christ will reign for a thousand years, and men will indulge in the carnal pleasures of the table. Hence they are called 'Chiliastae,'*[40] or believers in the Millennium.

The fables of the Jews and Mohammedans are also refuted, who pretend that the reward of the righteous consists in such pleasures. For happiness is the reward of virtue.

That Happiness Does Not Consist in Honors

From the foregoing it is also clear that neither does man's highest good, or happiness, consist in honors.

For man's ultimate end and happiness is his most perfect operation, as we have shown above.[41] But man's honor does not consist in some-

38. Cf. Aristotle, *Eth.*, I, 12 (1101b 14).
39. ["That All Things Are Directed . . ." Eds.]
40. St. Augustine, *De Haeres.*, 8 (PL 42, 27).
41. ["That to Know God Is the End" Eds.]

thing done by him, but in something done to him by another who shows him respect.[42] Therefore man's happiness must not be placed in honors.

Again. That which is for the sake of another good and desirable thing is not the last end. Now such is honor, for a man is not rightly honored, except because of some other good in him. For this reason men seek to be honored, as though wishing to have a voucher for some good that is in them; so that they rejoice more in being honored by the great and the wise. Therefore we must not assign man's happiness to honors.

Besides. Happiness is obtained through virtue. Now virtuous deeds are voluntary, or else they would not be praiseworthy. Therefore happiness must be a good obtainable by man through his will. But it is not in a man's power to secure honor, rather is it in the power of the man who pays honor. Therefore happiness is not to be assigned to honors.

Moreover. Only the good can be worthy of honor, and yet it is possible even for the wicked to be honored. Therefore it is better to become worthy of honor, than to be honored. Therefore honor is not man's supreme good.

Furthermore. The highest good is the perfect good. Now the perfect good is incompatible with any evil. But that which has no evil in it cannot possibly be evil. Therefore that which is in possession of the highest good cannot be evil. Yet it is possible for an evil person to receive honor. Therefore honor is not man's supreme good.

That Man's Happiness Does Not Consist in Glory

Therefore it is evident also that man's supreme good does not consist in glory, which is the recognition of one's good name.

For glory, according to Cicero, is *the general recognition and praise of a person's good name,*[43] and, in the words of Ambrose, consists in *being well known and praised.*[44] Now men seek praise and distinction through being famous, so that they may be honored by those whom their fame reaches. Therefore glory is sought for the sake of honor, and consequently if honor be not the highest good, much less is glory.

42. Cf. Aristotle, *Eth.*, I, 5 (1095b 25).
43. *De Inventione*, II, 55 (p. 150^b).
44. Cf. St. Augustine, *Contra Maximin.*, II, 13 (PL 42, 770).

Again. Those goods are worthy of praise, whereby a man shows himself to be ordered to his end. Now he who is directed to his end has not yet reached his last end. Therefore praise is not bestowed on one who has reached his last end; rather does he receive honor, as the Philosopher says.[45] Therefore glory cannot be the highest good, since it consists chiefly in praise.

Besides. It is better to know than to be known, because only the higher realities know, whereas the lowest are known. Therefore man's highest good cannot be glory, which consists in a man's being known.

Further. A man does not seek to be known except in good things; in evil things he seeks to be hidden. Therefore, to be known is good and desirable, because of the good things that are known in a man. Therefore these good things are better still. Consequently glory, which consists in a man's being known, is not his highest good.

Moreover. The highest good must needs be perfect, for it satisfies the appetite. But the knowledge of one's good name, wherein glory consists, is imperfect, for it is beset with much uncertainty and error. Therefore glory of this kind cannot be the supreme good.

Furthermore. Man's highest good must be supremely stable in human things, for it is natural to desire unfailing endurance in one's goods. Now glory, which consists in fame, is most unstable, since nothing is more changeable than human opinion and praise. Therefore such glory is not man's highest good.

That Man's Happiness Does Not Consist in Wealth

Hence it is evident that neither is wealth man's highest good. For wealth is not sought except for the sake of something else, because of itself it brings us no good, but only when we use it, whether for the support of the body or for some similar purpose. Now the highest good is sought for its own, and not for another's sake. Therefore wealth is not man's highest good.

Again. Man's highest good cannot consist in the possession or preservation of things whose chief advantage for man consists in their being spent. Now the chief advantage of wealth is in its being spent, for this is its use. Therefore the possession of wealth cannot be man's highest good.

45. *Eth.*, I, 12 (1101b 24).

Moreover. Acts of virtue deserve praise according as they lead to happiness. Now acts of liberality and magnificence, which are concerned with money, are deserving of praise because of money being spent rather than because of its being kept; and it is from this that these virtues derive their names. Therefore man's happiness does not consist in the possession of wealth.

Besides. Man's highest good must consist in obtaining something better than man. But man is better than wealth, since wealth is something directed to man's use. Therefore man's supreme good does not consist in wealth.

Further. Man's highest good is not subject to fortune.[46] For things that are fortuitous escape the forethought of reason, whereas man has to attain his own end by means of his reason. But fortune occupies the greatest place in the attaining of wealth. Therefore human happiness does not consist in wealth.

Moreover. This is evident from the fact that wealth is lost unwillingly; also because wealth can come into the possession of evil persons, who, of necessity, must lack the highest good. Again because wealth is unstable. Other similar reasons can be gathered from the arguments given above.[47]

That Happiness Does Not Consist in Worldly Power

In like manner, neither can worldly power be man's highest happiness, since in the achievement thereof chance can effect much. Again, it is unstable, and not subject to man's will; and it is often obtained by evil men. These are incompatible with the highest good, as was already stated.[48]

Again. Man is said to be good especially according as he approaches the highest good. But in respect to his having power, he is not said to be either good or evil, since not everyone who can do good deeds is good, nor is a person evil because he can do evil deeds. Therefore the highest good does not consist in being powerful.

Besides. Every power implies reference to something else. But the highest good is not referred to anything further. Therefore power is not man's highest good.

46. *Eth.*, I, 9 (1099b 24).
47. ["That Happiness Does Not Consist in Honors" ff. Eds.]
48. ["That Happiness Does Not Consist in Honors" ff. Eds.]

Moreover. Man's highest good cannot be a thing that one can use both well and ill; for the better things are those that we cannot abuse. But one can use one's power both well and ill, for *rational powers can be directed to contrary objects.*[49] Therefore human power is not man's good.

Further. If any power be man's highest good, it must be most perfect. Now human power is most imperfect, for it is based on human will and opinion, which are full of inconstancies. Also, the greater a power is reputed to be, the greater number of people does it depend on; which again conduces to its weakness, since what depends on many is in many ways destructible. Therefore man's highest good does not consist in worldly power.

Consequently man's happiness does not consist in any external good, for all external goods, which are known as *fortuitous goods*, are contained under those we have mentioned.[50]

That Happiness Does Not Consist in Goods of the Body

Like arguments avail to prove that man's highest good does not consist in goods of the body, such as health, beauty and strength. For they are common to good and evil, they are unstable, and they are not subject to the will.

Besides. The soul is better than the body, which neither lives nor possesses these goods without the soul. Therefore, the soul's good, such as understanding and the like, is better than the body's good. Therefore the body's good is not man's highest good.

Again. These goods are common to man and other animals, whereas happiness is a good proper to man. Therefore man's happiness does not consist in the things mentioned.

Moreover. Many animals surpass man in goods of the body, for some are fleeter than he, some more sturdy, and so on. Accordingly, if man's highest good consisted in these things, man would not excel all animals; which is clearly untrue. Therefore human happiness does not consist in goods of the body.

---

49. Aristotle, *Metaph.*, IX, 2 (1046b 25).
50. ["That Happiness Does Not Consist in Honors" ff. Eds.]

That Human Happiness Is Not Seated in the Senses

By the same arguments it is evident that neither does man's highest good consist in goods of his sensitive nature. For these goods, again, are common to man and other animals.

Again. Intellect is superior to sense. Therefore the intellect's good is better than that of the sense. Consequently man's supreme good is not seated in the senses.

Besides. The greatest sensual pleasures are those of the table and of sex, wherein the supreme good must needs be, if seated in the senses. But it does not consist in them. Therefore man's highest good is not in the senses.

Moreover. The senses are appreciated for their utility and for knowledge. Now the entire utility of the senses is referred to the goods of the body. Again, sensitive knowledge is ordered to intellectual knowledge, and hence animals devoid of intellect take no pleasure in sensation except in reference to some bodily utility, in so far as by sensitive knowledge they obtain food or sexual intercourse. Therefore, man's highest good which is happiness is not seated in the sensitive part of man.

That Man's Ultimate Happiness Does Not Consist in Acts of the Moral Virtues

It is clear that man's ultimate happiness does not consist in moral activities.

For human happiness, if ultimate, cannot be directed to a further end. But all moral activities can be directed to something else. This is clear from a consideration of the principal among them. Because deeds of fortitude in time of war are directed to victory and peace; for it were foolish to go to war merely for its own sake.[51] Again, deeds of justice are directed to keeping peace among men, for each man possesses with contentment what is his own. The same applies to all the other virtues. Therefore man's ultimate happiness is not in moral deeds.

Again. The purpose of the moral virtues is that through them we may observe the mean in the passions within us, and in things outside

51. Cf. Aristotle, *Eth.*, X, 7 (1177b 9).

us. Now it is impossible that the moderation of passions or of external things be the ultimate end of man's life, since both passions and external things can be directed to something less. Therefore it is not possible that the practice of moral virtue be man's final happiness.

Further. Since man is man through the possession of reason, his proper good, which is happiness, must needs be in accordance with that which is proper to reason. Now that which reason has in itself is more proper to reason than what it effects in something else. Seeing, then, that the good of moral virtue is a good established by reason in something other than itself, it cannot be the greatest good of man which happiness is; rather this good must be a good that is in reason itself.

Moreover. We have already proved that the last end of all things is to become like God.[52] Therefore that in which man chiefly becomes like God will be his happiness. Now this is not in terms of moral actions, since such actions cannot be ascribed to God, except metaphorically: for it is not befitting to God to have passions, or the like, with which moral virtue is concerned. Therefore man's ultimate happiness, which is his last end, does not consist in moral actions.

Furthermore. Happiness is man's proper good. Therefore that good, which of all goods is most proper to man in comparison with other animals, is the one in which we must seek his ultimate happiness. Now this is not the practice of moral virtue, for animals share somewhat either in liberality or in fortitude, whereas no animal has a share in intellectual activity. Therefore man's ultimate happiness does not consist in moral acts.

That Ultimate Happiness Does Not Consist in the Act of Prudence

It is also evident from the foregoing that neither does man's happiness consist in the act of prudence.

For acts of prudence are solely about matters of moral virtue. But human happiness does not consist in the practice of moral virtue.[53] Neither therefore does it consist in the practice of prudence.

Again. Man's ultimate happiness consists in man's most excellent

52. ["That All Things Tend to Be Like unto God" Eds.]
53. ["That Man's Ultimate Happiness Does Not Consist in Acts of the Moral Virtues" Eds.]

operation. Now man's most excellent operation, in terms of what is proper to man, is in relation to most perfect objects. But the act of prudence is not concerned with the most perfect objects of intellect or reason; for it is not about necessary things, but about contingent practical matters.[54] Therefore its act is not man's ultimate happiness.

Besides. That which is ordered to another as to its end is not man's ultimate happiness. Now the act of prudence is ordered to another as to its end, both because all practical knowledge, under which prudence is comprised, is ordered to operation, and because prudence disposes a man well in choosing means to an end, as may be gathered from Aristotle.[55] Therefore man's ultimate happiness is not in the practice of prudence.

Furthermore. Irrational animals have no share of happiness, as Aristotle proves.[56] Yet some of them have a certain share of prudence, as may be gathered from the same author.[57] Therefore happiness does not consist in an act of prudence.

That Happiness Does Not Consist in the Practice of Art

It is also evident that it cannot consist in the practice of art.

For even the knowledge of art is practical, and so is directed to an end, and is not the ultimate end.

Besides. The end of the practice of art is the thing produced by art, and such a thing cannot be the ultimate end of human life, since it is rather we who are the end of those products, for they are all made for man's use. Therefore final happiness cannot consist in the practice of art.

That Man's Ultimate Happiness Consists in Contemplating God

Accordingly, if man's ultimate happiness does not consist in external things, which are called goods of fortune; nor in goods of the body; nor in goods of the soul, as regards the sensitive part; nor as regards the intellectual part, in terms of the life of moral virtue; nor in terms

54. Cf. Aristotle, *Eth.*, VI, 5 (1104a 35).
55. *Op. cit.*, VI, 13 (1145a 6).
56. *Op. cit.*, I, 9 (1099b 33).
57. Aristotle, *Metaph.*, I, 1 (980a 30).

of the intellectual virtues which are concerned with action, namely, art and prudence:—it remains for us to conclude that man's ultimate happiness consists in the contemplation of truth.

For this operation alone is proper to man, and it is in it that none of the other animals communicates.

Again. This is not directed to anything further as to its end, since the contemplation of the truth is sought for its own sake.

Again. By this operation man is united to beings above him, by becoming like them; because of all human actions this alone is both in God and in the separate substances. Also, by this operation man comes into contact with those higher beings, through knowing them in any way whatever.

Besides, man is more self-sufficing for this operation, seeing that he stands in little need of the help of external things in order to perform it.

Further. All other human operations seem to be ordered to this as to their end. For perfect contemplation requires that the body should be disencumbered, and to this effect are directed all the products of art that are necessary for life. Moreover, it requires freedom from the disturbance caused by the passions, which is achieved by means of the moral virtues and of prudence; and freedom from external disturbance, to which the whole governance of the civil life is directed. So that, if we consider the matter rightly, we shall see that all human occupations appear to serve those who contemplate the truth.

Now, it is not possible that man's ultimate happiness consist in contemplation based on the understanding of first principles; for this is most imperfect, as being most universal, containing potentially the knowledge of things. Moreover, it is the beginning and not the end of human inquiry, and comes to us from nature, and not through the pursuit of the truth. Nor does it consist in contemplation based on the sciences that have the lowest things for their object, since happiness must consist in an operation of the intellect in relation to the most noble intelligible objects. It follows then that man's ultimate happiness consists in wisdom, based on the consideration of divine things.

It is therefore evident also by way of induction that man's ultimate happiness consists solely in the contemplation of God, which conclusion was proved above by arguments.[58]

58. ["That to Know God Is the End" Eds.]

6

Friedrich Nietzsche, "The Madman" and "Eternal Recurrence," from *The Gay Science*

Friedrich Nietzsche (1844–1900), German philosopher and poet, attempted to elaborate the full implications of atheism, proposing new "post-Christian" myths, such as those in the two texts that follow.

The madman.—Have you not heard of that madman who lit a lantern in the bright morning hours, ran to the market place, and cried incessantly: "I seek God! I seek God!"—As many of those who did not believe in God were standing around just then, he provoked much laughter. Has he got lost? asked one. Did he lose his way like a child? asked another. Or is he hiding? Is he afraid of us? Has he gone on a voyage? emigrated?—Thus they yelled and laughed.

The madman jumped into their midst and pierced them with his eyes. "Whither is God?" he cried; "I will tell you. *We have killed him*—you and I. All of us are his murderers. But how did we do this? How could we drink up the sea? Who gave us the sponge to wipe away the entire horizon? What were we doing when we unchained this earth from its sun? Whither is it moving now? Whither are we moving? Away from all suns? Are we not plunging continually? Backward, sideward, forward, in all directions? Is there still any up or down? Are we not straying as through an infinite nothing? Do we not feel the breath of empty space? Has it not become colder? Is not night continually closing in on us? Do we not need to light lanterns in the morning? Do we hear nothing as yet of the noise of the gravediggers who are burying God? Do we smell nothing as yet of the divine decomposition? Gods, too, decompose. God is dead. God remains dead. And we have killed him.

"How shall we comfort ourselves, the murderers of all murderers? What was holiest and mightiest of all that the world has yet owned has bled to death under our knives: who will wipe this blood off us? What

Nietzsche, *The Gay Science*, trans. Walter Kaufman, Penguin, New York, 1974.

water is there for us to clean ourselves? What festivals of atonement, what sacred games shall we have to invent? Is not the greatness of this deed too great for us? Must we ourselves not become gods simply to appear worthy of it? There has never been a greater deed; and whoever is born after us—for the sake of this deed he will belong to a higher history than all history hitherto."

Here the madman fell silent and looked again at his listeners; and they, too, were silent and stared at him in astonishment. At last he threw his lantern on the ground, and it broke into pieces and went out. "I have come too early," he said then; "my time is not yet. This tremendous event is still on its way, still wandering; it has not yet reached the ears of men. Lightning and thunder require time; the light of the stars requires time; deeds, though done, still require time to be seen and heard. This deed is still more distant from them than the most distant stars—*and yet they have done it themselves.*"

It has been related further that on the same day the madman forced his way into several churches and there struck up his *requiem aeternam deo.* Led out and called to account, he is said always to have replied nothing but: "What after all are these churches now if they are not the tombs and sepulchers of God?"

The greatest weight.—What, if some day or night a demon were to steal after you into your loneliest loneliness and say to you: "This life as you now live it and have lived it you will have to live once more and innumerable times more; and there will be nothing new in it, but every pain and every joy and every thought and sigh and everything unutterably small or great in your life will have to return to you, all in the same succession and sequence—even this spider and this moonlight between the trees, and even this moment and I myself. The eternal hourglass of existence is turned upside down again and again, and you with it, speck of dust!"

Would you not throw yourself down and gnash your teeth and curse the demon who spoke thus? Or have you once experienced a tremendous moment when you would have answered him: "You are a god and never have I heard anything more divine." If this thought gained possession of you, it would change you as you are or perhaps crush you. The question in each and every thing, "Do you desire this once more and innumerable times more?" would lie upon your actions as the greatest weight. Or how well disposed would you have to become to yourself and to life *to crave nothing more fervently* than this ultimate eternal confirmation and seal?

7

Jean-Paul Sartre, "Mysticism of the Absurd," from *Nausea*

Jean-Paul Sartre (1905–1980), French philosopher, playwright, and novelist, was particularly interested in the question of human freedom and its relation to social ethics. His most important philosophical works are Being and Nothingness *and the* Critique of Dialectical Reason. *In our text from the novel* Nausea, *Rôquentin, a young French historian, has a strange apprehension concerning his existence.*

I can't say I feel relieved or satisfied; just the opposite, I am crushed. Only my goal is reached: I know what I wanted to know; I have understood all that has happened to me since January. The Nausea has not left me and I don't believe it will leave me so soon; but I no longer have to bear it, it is no longer an illness or a passing fit: it is I.

So I was in the park just now. The roots of the chestnut tree were sunk in the ground just under my bench. I couldn't remember it was a root any more. The words had vanished and with them the significance of things, their methods of use, and the feeble points of reference which men have traced on their surface. I was sitting, stooping forward, head bowed, alone in front of this black, knotty mass, entirely beastly, which frightened me. Then I had this vision.

It left me breathless. Never, until these last few days, had I understood the meaning of "existence." I was like the others, like the ones walking along the seashore, all dressed in their spring finery. I said, like them, "The ocean *is* green; that white speck up there *is* a seagull," but I didn't feel that it existed or that the seagull was an "existing seagull"; usually existence hides itself. It is there, around us, in us, it is *us*, you can't say two words without mentioning it, but you can never touch it. When I believed I was thinking about it, I must believe that I was thinking nothing, my head was empty, or there was just one word

Sartre, *Nausea*, New Directions, New York, 1969.

in my head, the word "to be." Or else I was thinking . . . how can I explain it? I was thinking of *belonging,* I was telling myself that the sea belonged to the class of green objects, or that the green was a part of the quality of the sea. Even when I looked at things, I was miles from dreaming that they existed: they looked like scenery to me. I picked them up in my hands, they served me as tools, I foresaw their resistance. But that all happened on the surface. If anyone had asked me what existence was, I would have answered, in good faith, that it was nothing, simply an empty form which was added to external things without changing anything in their nature. And then all of a sudden, there it was, clear as day: existence had suddenly unveiled itself. It had lost the harmless look of an abstract category: it was the very paste of things, this root was kneaded into existence. Or rather the root, the park gates, the bench, the sparse grass, all that had vanished: the diversity of things, their individuality, were only an appearance, a veneer. This veneer had melted, leaving soft, monstrous masses, all in disorder—naked, in a frightful, obscene nakedness.

I kept myself from making the slightest movement, but I didn't need to move in order to see, behind the trees, the blue columns and the lamp posts of the bandstand and the Velleda, in the midst of a mountain of laurel. All these objects . . . how can I explain? They inconvenienced me; I would have liked them to exist less strongly, more dryly, in a more abstract way, with more reserve. The chestnut tree pressed itself against my eyes. Green rust covered it half-way up; the bark, black and swollen, looked like boiled leather. The sound of the water in the Masqueret Fountain sounded in my ears, made a nest there, filled them with signs; my nostrils overflowed with a green, putrid odour. All things, gently, tenderly, were letting themselves drift into existence like those relaxed women who burst out laughing and say: "It's good to laugh," in a wet voice; they were parading, one in front of the other, exchanging abject secrets about their existence. I realized that there was no half-way house between non-existence and this flaunting abundance. If you existed, you had to *exist all the way,* as far as mouldiness, bloatedness, obscenity were concerned. In another world, circles, bars of music keep their pure and rigid lines. But existence is a deflection. Trees, night-blue pillars, the happy bubbling of a fountain, vital smells, little heat-mists floating in the cold air, a red-haired man digesting on a bench: all this somnolence, all these meals digested together, had its comic side. . . . Comic . . . no: it didn't go as far as that, nothing that exists can be comic; it was like a floating analogy, almost entirely elusive, with certain aspects of vaudeville. We were a heap of living creatures, irritated, embarrassed at ourselves, we hadn't the slightest reason to be there, none of us, each one, confused, vaguely alarmed, felt in the way in relation to the others. *In the way:* it was the only relationship I could establish between these trees, these gates, these stones. In vain I tried to *count* the chestnut trees, to *locate* them by their relationship to the Velleda, to compare their height with the height of the plane trees: each of them escaped the relationship in which I tried to enclose it, isolated itself, and overflowed. Of these relations (which I insisted on maintaining in order to delay the crumbling of the human world, measures, quantities, and directions)—I felt myself to be the arbitrator; they no longer had their teeth into things. *In the way*, the chestnut tree there, opposite me, a little to the left. *In the way*, the Velleda. . . .'

And I—soft, weak, obscene, digesting, juggling with dismal thoughts—I, too, was *In the way*. Fortunately, I didn't feel it, although I realized it, but I was uncomfortable because I was afraid of feeling it (even now I am afraid—afraid that it might catch me behind my head and lift me up like a wave). I dreamed vaguely of killing myself to wipe out at least one of these superfluous lives. But even my death would have been *In the way*. *In the way*, my corpse, my blood on these stones, between these plants, at the back of this smiling garden. And the decomposed flesh would have been *In the way* in the earth which would receive my bones, at last, cleaned, stripped, peeled, proper and clean as teeth, it would have been *In the way:* I was *In the way* for eternity.

The word absurdity is coming to life under my pen; a little while ago, in the garden, I couldn't find it, but neither was I looking for it, I didn't need it: I thought without words, *on* things, *with* things. Absurdity was not an idea in my head, or the sound of a voice, only this long serpent dead at my feet, this wooden serpent. Serpent or claw or root or vulture's talon, what difference does it make. And without formulating anything clearly. I understood that I had found the key to Existence, the key to my Nauseas, to my own life. In fact, all that I could grasp beyond that returns to this fundamental absurdity. Absurdity: another word; I struggle against words; down there I touched the thing. But I wanted to fix the absolute character of this absurdity here. A movement, an event in the tiny coloured world of men is only relatively absurd: by relation to the accompanying circumstances. A madman's ravings, for example, are absurd in relation to the situation in which he finds himself, but not in relation to his delirium. But a little while ago I made an experiment with the absolute or the absurd. This root—there was nothing in relation to which it was absurd. Oh, how can I put it in words? Absurd: in relation to the stones, the tufts of yellow grass, the dry mud, the tree, the sky, the green benches. Absurd, irreducible; nothing—not even a profound, secret upheaval of nature—could explain it. Evidently I did not know everything, I had not seen the seeds sprout, or the tree grow. But faced with this great wrinkled paw, neither ignorance nor knowledge was important: the world of explanations and reasons is not the world of existence. A circle is not absurd, it is clearly explained by the rotation of a straight segment around one of its extremities. But neither does a circle exist. This root, on the other hand, existed in such a way that I could not explain it. Knotty, inert, nameless, it fascinated me, filled my eyes, brought me back unceasingly to its own existence. In vain to repeat: "This is a root"—it didn't work any more. I saw clearly that you could not pass from its function as a root, as a breathing pump, *to that*, to this hard and compact skin of a sea lion, to this oily, callous, headstrong look. The function explained nothing: it allowed you to understand generally that it was a root, but not *that one* at all. This root, with its colour, shape, its congealed movement, was . . . below all explanation. Each of its qualities escaped it a little, flowed out of it, half solidified, almost became a thing; each one was *In the way* in the root and the whole stump now gave me the impression of unwinding itself a little, denying its existence to lose itself in a frenzied excess. I scraped my heel against this black claw: I wanted to peel off some of the bark. For no reason at all, out of defiance, to make the bare pink appear absurd on the tanned leather: to *play* with the absurdity of the world. But, when I drew my heel back, I saw that the bark was still black.

Black? I felt the word deflating, emptied of meaning with extraordinary rapidity. Black? The root *was not* black, there was no black on this piece of wood—there was . . . something else: black, like the circle, did not exist. I looked at the root: was it *more than* black or *almost* black? But I soon stopped questioning myself because I had the feeling of knowing where I was. Yes, I had already scrutinized innumerable objects, with deep uneasiness. I had already tried—vainly—to think something *about* them: and I had already felt their cold, inert qualities elude me, slip through my fingers. Adolphe's suspenders, the other evening in the "Railwaymen's Rendezvous." They *were not* purple. I saw the two inexplicable stains on the shirt. And the stone—the well-known stone, the origin of this whole business: it was not . . . I can't remember exactly just what it was that the stone refused to be. But I had not forgotten its passive resistance. And the hand of the Self-Taught Man; I held it and shook it one day in the library and then I had the feeling that it wasn't quite a hand. I had thought of a great white worm, but that wasn't it either. And the suspicious transparency of the glass of beer in the Café Mably. Suspicious: that's what they were, the sounds, the smells, the tastes. When they ran quickly under your nose like startled hares and you didn't pay too much attention, you might believe them to be simple and reassuring, you might believe that there was real blue in the world, real red, a real perfume of almonds or violets. But as soon as you held on to them for an instant, this feeling of comfort and security gave way to a deep uneasiness: colours, tastes, and smells were never real, never themselves and nothing but themselves. The simplest, most indefinable quality had too much content, in relation to itself, in its heart. That black against my foot, it didn't look like black, but rather the confused effort to imagine black by someone who had never seen black and who wouldn't know how to stop, who would have imagined an ambiguous being beyond colours. It *looked* like a colour, but also . . . like a bruise or a secretion, like an oozing—and something else, an odour, for example, it melted into the odour of wet earth, warm, moist wood, into a black odour that spread like varnish over this sensitive wood, in a flavour of chewed, sweet fibre. I did not simply *see* this black: sight is an abstract invention, a simplified idea, one of man's ideas. That black, amorphous, weakly presence, far surpassed sight, smell and taste. But this richness was lost in confusion and finally was no more because it was too much.

This moment was extraordinary. I was there, motionless and icy, plunged in a horrible ecstasy. But something fresh had just appeared in the very heart of this ecstasy; I understood the Nausea, I possessed it. To tell the truth, I did not formulate my discoveries to myself. But I think it would be easy for me to put them in words now. The essential thing is contingency. I mean that one cannot define existence as necessary. To exist is simply *to be there;* those who exist let themselves be encountered, but you can never deduce anything from them. I believe there are people who have understood this. Only they tried to overcome this contingency by inventing a necessary, causal being. But no necessary being can explain existence: contingency is not a delusion, a probability which can be dissipated; it is the absolute, consequently, the perfect free gift. All is free, this park, this city and myself. When you realize that, it turns your heart upside down and everything begins to float, as the other evening at the "Railwaymen's Rendezvous": here is Nausea; here there is what those bastards—the ones on the Coteau Vert and others—try to hide from themselves with their idea of their rights. But what a poor lie: no one has any rights; they are entirely free, like other men, they cannot succeed in not feeling superfluous. And in themselves, secretly, they are *superfluous,* that is to say, amorphous, vague, and sad.

How long will this fascination last? I *was* the root of the chestnut tree. Or rather I was entirely conscious of its existence. Still detached from it—since I was conscious of it—yet lost in it, nothing but it. An uneasy conscience which, notwithstanding, let itself fall with all its weight on this piece of dead wood. Time had stopped: a small black pool at my feet; it was impossible for something to come *after* that moment. I would have liked to tear myself from that atrocious joy, but I did not even imagine it would be possible; I was inside; the black stump did *not move,* it stayed there, in my eyes, as a lump of food sticks in the windpipe. I could neither accept nor refuse it. At what a cost did I raise my eyes? Did I raise them? Rather did I not obliterate myself for an instant in order to be reborn in the following instant with my head thrown back and my eyes raised upward? In fact, I was not even conscious of the transformation. But suddenly it became impossible for me to think of the existence of the root. It was wiped out, I could repeat in vain: it exists, it is still there, under the bench, against my right foot, it no longer meant anything. Existence is not something which lets itself be thought of from a distance: it must invade you suddenly, master you, weigh heavily on your heart like a great motionless beast—or else there is nothing more at all.

There was nothing more, my eyes were empty and I was spellbound by my deliverance. Then suddenly it began to move before my eyes in light, uncertain motions: the wind was shaking the top of the tree.

It did not displease me to see a movement, it was a change from these motionless beings who watched me like staring eyes. I told myself, as I followed the swinging of the branches: movements never quite exist, they are passages, intermediaries between two existences, moments of weakness, I expected to see them come out of nothingness, progressively ripen, blossom: I was finally going to surprise beings in the process of being born.

No more than three seconds, and all my hopes were swept away. I could not attribute the passage of time to these branches groping around like blind men. This idea of passage was still an invention of man. The idea was too transparent. All these paltry agitations, drew in on themselves, isolated. They overflowed the leaves and branches everywhere. They whirled about these empty hands, enveloped them with tiny whirlwinds. Of course a movement was something different from a tree. But it was still an absolute. A thing. My eyes only encountered completion. The tips of the branches rustled with existence which unceasingly renewed itself and which was never born. The existing wind rested on the tree like a great bluebottle, and the tree shuddered. But the shudder was not a nascent quality, a passing from power to action; it was a thing; a shudder-thing flowed into the tree, took possession of it, shook it and suddenly abandoned it, going further on to spin about itself. All was fullness and all was active, there was no weakness in time, all, even the least perceptible stirring, was made of existence. And all these existents which bustled about this tree came from nowhere and were going nowhere. Suddenly they existed, then suddenly they existed no longer: existence is without memory; of the vanished it retains nothing—not even a memory. Existence everywhere, infinitely, in excess, for ever and everywhere; existence—which is limited only by existence. I sank down on the bench, stupefied, stunned by this profusion of beings without origin: everywhere blossomings, hatchings out, my ears buzzed with existence, my very flesh throbbed and opened, abandoned itself to the universal burgeoning. It was repugnant. But why, I thought, why so many existences, since they all look alike? What good are so many duplicates of trees? So many existences missed, obstinately begun again and again missed—like the awkward efforts of an insect fallen on its back? (I was one of those efforts.) That abundance did not give the effect of generosity, just the opposite. It was dismal, ailing, embarrassed at itself. Those trees, those great clumsy bodies. . . . I began to laugh because I suddenly thought of the formidable springs described in books, full of crackings, burstings, gigantic explosions. There were those idiots who came to tell you about willpower and struggle for life. Hadn't they ever seen a beast or a tree? This plane-tree with its scaling bark, this half-rotten oak, they wanted me to take them for rugged youthful endeavour surging towards the sky. And that root? I would have undoubtedly had to represent it as a voracious claw tearing at the earth, devouring its food?

Impossible to see things that way. Weaknesses, frailties, yes. The trees floated. Gushing towards the sky? Or rather a collapse; at any instant I expected to see the tree-trunks shrivel like weary wands, crumple up, fall on the ground in a soft, folded, black heap. *They did not want* to exist, only they could not help themselves. So they quietly minded their own business; the sap rose up slowly through the structure, half reluctant, and the roots sank slowly into the earth. But at each instant they seemed on the verge of leaving everything there and obliterating themselves. Tired and old, they kept on existing, against the grain, simply because they were too weak to die, because death could only come to them from the outside: strains of music alone can proudly carry their own death within themselves like an internal necessity: only they don't exist. Every existing thing is born without reason, prolongs itself out of weakness and dies by chance. I leaned back and closed my eyes. But the images, forewarned, immediately leaped up and filled my closed eyes with existences: existence is a fullness which man can never abandon.

Strange images. They represented a multitude of things. Not real things, other things which looked like them. Wooden objects which looked like chairs, shoes, other objects which looked like plants. And then two faces: the couple who were eating opposite to me last Sunday in the Brasserie Vézelise. Fat, hot, sensual, absurd, with red ears. I could see the woman's neck and shoulders. Nude existence. Those two—it suddenly gave me a turn—those two were still existing somewhere in Bouville; somewhere—in the midst of smells?—this soft throat rubbing up luxuriously against smooth stuffs, nestling in lace; and the woman picturing her bosom under her blouse, thinking: "My titties, my lovely fruits," smiling mysteriously, attentive to the swelling of her breasts which tickled . . . then I shouted and found myself with my eyes wide open.

Had I dreamed of this enormous presence? It was there, in the garden, toppled down into the trees, all soft, sticky, soiling everything, all thick, a jelly. And I was inside, I with the garden. I was frightened, furious, I thought it was so stupid, so out of place, I hated this ignoble mess. Mounting up, mounting up as high as the sky, spilling over, filling everything with its gelatinous slither, and I could see depths upon depths of it reaching far beyond the limits of the garden, the houses, and Bouville, as far as the eye could reach. I was no longer in Bouville, I was nowhere, I was floating. I was not surprised, I knew it was the World, the naked World suddenly revealing itself, and I choked with rage at this gross, absurd being. You couldn't even wonder where all that sprang from, or how it was that a world came into existence, rather than nothingness. It didn't make sense, the World was everywhere, in front, behind. There had been nothing *before* it. Nothing. There had never been a moment in which it could not have existed. That was what worried me: of course there was no *reason* for this flowing larva to exist. *But it was impossible* for it not to exist. It was unthinkable: to imagine nothingness you had to be there already, in the midst of the World eyes wide open and alive; nothingness was only an idea in my head, an existing idea floating in this immensity: this nothingness had not come *before* existence, it was an existence like any other and appeared after many others. I shouted "filth! what rotten filth!" and shook myself to get rid of this sticky filth, but it held fast and there was so much, tons and tons of existence, endless: I stifled at the depths of this immense weariness. And then suddenly the park emptied as through a great hole, the World disappeared as it had come, or else I woke up—in any case, I saw no more of it; nothing was left but the yellow earth around me, out of which dead branches rose upward.

I got up and went out. Once at the gate, I turned back. Then the garden smiled at me. I leaned against the gate and watched for a long time. The smile of the trees, of the laurel, *meant* something; that was the real secret of existence. I remembered one Sunday, not more than three weeks ago, I had already detected everywhere a sort of conspiratorial air. Was it in my intention? I felt with boredom that I had no way of understanding. No way. Yet it was there, waiting, looking at one. It was there on the trunk of the chestnut tree . . . it was *the* chestnut tree. Things—you might have called them thoughts—which stopped halfway, which were forgotten, which forgot what they wanted to think and which stayed like that, hanging about with an odd little sense which was beyond them. That little sense annoyed me: I *could not* understand it, even if I could have stayed leaning against the gate for a century; I had learned all I could know about existence. I left, I went back to the hotel and I wrote.

.   .   .

8

Albert Camus,
"Absurdity Is the Divorce between Reason and the World,"
from *The Myth of Sisyphus* and *Nuptials*

Albert Camus (1913–1960), philosopher and novelist, was born in North Africa and settled in Paris, where he was active in the Resistance. His central theme is the emergence of beauty and heroism against a background of absurdity.

Philosophical Suicide

All great deeds and all great thoughts have a ridiculous beginning. Great works are often born on a streetcorner or in a restaurant's revolving door. So it is with absurdity. The absurd world more than others derives its nobility from that abject birth. In certain situations, replying "nothing" when asked what one is thinking about may be pretense in a man. Those who are loved are well aware of this. But if that reply is sincere, if it symbolizes that odd state of soul in which the void becomes eloquent, in which the chain of daily gestures is broken, in which the heart vainly seeks the link that will connect it again, then it is as it were the first sign of absurdity.

It happens that the stage sets collapse. Rising, streetcar, four hours in the office or the factory, meal, streetcar, four hours of work, meal, sleep, and Monday Tuesday Wednesday Thursday Friday and Saturday according to the same rhythm—this path is easily followed most of the time. But one day the "why" arises and everything begins in that weariness tinged with amazement. "Begins"—this is important. Weariness comes at the end of the acts of a mechanical life, but at the

Camus, *The Myth of Sisyphus and Other Essays*, trans. Justin O'Brien, New York, Alfred A. Knopf, 1969.

same time it inaugurates the impulse of consciousness. It awakens consciousness and provokes what follows. What follows is the gradual return into the chain or it is the definitive awakening. At the end of the awakening comes, in time, the consequence: suicide or recovery. In itself weariness has something sickening about it. Here, I must conclude that it is good. For everything begins with consciousness and nothing is worth anything except through it. There is nothing original about these remarks. But they are obvious; that is enough for a while, during a sketchy reconnaissance in the origins of the absurd. Mere "anxiety," as Heidegger says, is at the source of everything.

Likewise and during every day of an unillustrious life, time carries us. But a moment always comes when we have to carry it. We live on the future: "tomorrow," "later on," "when you have made your way," "you will understand when you are old enough." Such irrelevancies are wonderful, for, after all, it's a matter of dying. Yet a day comes when a man notices or says that he is thirty. Thus he asserts his youth. But simultaneously he situates himself in relation to time. He takes his place in it. He admits that he stands at a certain point on a curve that he acknowledges having to travel to its end. He belongs to time, and by the horror that seizes him, he recognizes his worst enemy. Tomorrow, he was longing for tomorrow, whereas everything in him ought to reject it. That revolt of the flesh is the absurd.[1]

A step lower and strangeness creeps in: perceiving that the world is "dense," sensing to what a degree a stone is foreign and irreducible to us, with what intensity nature or a landscape can negate us. At the heart of all beauty lies something inhuman, and these hills, the softness of the sky, the outline of these trees at this very minute lose the illusory meaning with which we had clothed them, henceforth more remote than a lost paradise. The primitive hostility of the world rises up to face us across millennia. For a second we cease to understand it because for centuries we have understood in it solely the images and designs that we had attributed to it beforehand, because henceforth we lack the power to make use of that artifice. The world evades us because it becomes itself again. That stage scenery masked by habit becomes again what it is. It withdraws at a distance from us. Just as there are days when under the familiar face of a woman, we see as a stranger her we had loved months or years ago,

---

1. But not in the proper sense. This is not a definition, but rather an *enumeration* of the feelings that may admit of the absurd. Still, the enumeration finished, the absurd has nevertheless not been exhausted.

perhaps we shall come even to desire what suddenly leaves us so alone. But the time has not yet come. Just one thing: that denseness and that strangeness of the world is the absurd.

Men, too, secrete the inhuman. At certain moments of lucidity, the mechanical aspect of their gestures, their meaningless pantomime makes silly everything that surrounds them. A man is talking on the telephone behind a glass partition; you cannot hear him, but you see his incomprehensible dumb show: you wonder why he is alive. This discomfort in the face of man's own inhumanity, this incalculable tumble before the image of what we are, this "nausea," as a writer of today calls it, is also the absurd. Likewise the stranger who at certain seconds comes to meet us in a mirror, the familiar and yet alarming brother we encounter in our own photographs is also the absurd.

I come at last to death and to the attitude we have toward it. On this point everything has been said and it is only proper to avoid pathos. Yet one will never be sufficiently surprised that everyone lives as if no one "knew." This is because in reality there is no experience of death. Properly speaking, nothing has been experienced but what has been lived and made conscious. Here, it is barely possible to speak of the experience of others' deaths. It is a substitute, an illusion, and it never quite convinces us. That melancholy convention cannot be persuasive. The horror comes in reality from the mathematical aspect of the event. If time frightens us, this is because it works out the problem and the solution comes afterward. All the pretty speeches about the soul will have their contrary convincingly proved, at least for a time. From this inert body on which a slap makes no mark the soul has disappeared. This elementary and definitive aspect of the adventure constitutes the absurd feeling. Under the fatal lighting of that destiny, its uselessness becomes evident. No code of ethics and no effort are justifiable *a priori* in the face of the cruel mathematics that command our condition.

Let me repeat: all this has been said over and over. I am limiting myself here to making a rapid classification and to pointing out these obvious themes. They run through all literatures and all philosophies. Everyday conversation feeds on them. There is no question of rein-venting them. But it is essential to be sure of these facts in order to be able to question oneself subsequently on the primordial question. I am interested—let me repeat again—not so much in absurd discover-ies as in their consequences. If one is assured of these facts, what is one to conclude, how far is one to go to elude nothing? Is one to die voluntarily or to hope in spite of everything? Beforehand, it is necessary to take the same rapid inventory on the plane of the intelligence. The mind's first step is to distinguish what is true from what is false. However, as soon as thought reflects on itself, what it first discovers is a contradiction. Useless to strive to be convincing in this case. Over the centuries no one has furnished a clearer and more elegant demonstration of the business than Aristotle: "The often ridiculed consequence of these opinions is that they destroy themselves. For by asserting that all is true we assert the truth of the contrary assertion and consequently the falsity of our own thesis (for the contrary assertion does not admit that it can be true). And if one says that all is false, that assertion is itself false. If we declare that solely the assertion opposed to ours is false or else that solely ours is not false, we are nevertheless forced to admit an infinite number of true or false judgments. For the one who expresses a true assertion proclaims simultaneously that it is true, and so on *ad infinitum.*"

This vicious circle is but the first of a series in which the mind that studies itself gets lost in a giddy whirling. The very simplicity of these paradoxes makes them irreducible. Whatever may be the plays on words and the acrobatics of logic, to understand is, above all, to unify. The mind's deepest desire, even in its most elaborate operations, parallels man's unconscious feeling in the face of his universe: it is an insistence upon familiarity, an appetite for clarity. Understanding the world for a man is reducing it to the human, stamping it with his seal. The cat's universe is not the universe of the anthill. The truism "All thought is anthropomorphic" has no other meaning. Likewise, the mind that aims to understand reality can consider itself satisfied only by reducing it to terms of thought. If man realized that the universe like him can love and suffer, he would be reconciled. If thought discovered in the shimmering mirrors of phenomena eternal relations capable of summing them up and summing themselves up in a single principle, then would be seen an intellectual joy of which the myth of the blessed would be but a ridiculous imitation. That nostalgia for unity, that appetite for the absolute illustrates the essential impulse of the human drama. But the fact of that nostalgia's existence does not imply that it is to be immediately satisfied. For if, bridging the gulf that separates desire from conquest, we assert with Parmenides the reality of the One (whatever it may be), we fall into the ridiculous contradiction of a mind that asserts total unity and proves by its very assertion its own difference and the diversity it claimed to resolve. This other vicious circle is enough to stifle our hopes.

These are again truisms. I shall again repeat that they are not interesting in themselves but in the consequences that can be deduced from them. I know another truism: it tells me that man is mortal. One can nevertheless count the minds that have deduced the extreme conclusions from it. It is essential to consider as a constant point of reference in this essay the regular hiatus between what we fancy we know and what we really know, practical assent and simulated ignorance which allows us to live with ideas which, if we truly put them to the test, ought to upset our whole life. Faced with this inextricable contradiction of the mind, we shall fully grasp the divorce separating us from our own creations. So long as the mind keeps silent in the motionless world of its hopes, everything is reflected and arranged in the unity of its nostalgia. But with its first move this world cracks and tumbles: an infinite number of shimmering fragments is offered to the understanding. We must despair of ever reconstructing the familiar, calm surface which would give us peace of heart. After so many centuries of inquiries, so many abdications among thinkers, we are well aware that this is true for all our knowledge. With the exception of professional rationalists, today people despair of true knowledge. If the only significant history of human thought were to be written, it would have to be the history of its successive regrets and its impotences.

Of whom and of what indeed can I say: "I know that!" This heart within me I can feel, and I judge that it exists. This world I can touch, and I likewise judge that it exists. There ends all my knowledge, and the rest is construction. For if I try to seize this self of which I feel sure, if I try to define and to summarize it, it is nothing but water slipping through my fingers. I can sketch one by one all the aspects it is able to assume, all those likewise that have been attributed to it, this upbringing, this origin, this ardor or these silences, this nobility or this vileness. But aspects cannot be added up. This very heart which is mine will forever remain indefinable to me. Between the certainty I have of my existence and the content I try to give to that assurance, the gap will never be filled. Forever I shall be a stranger to myself. In psychology as in logic, there are truths but no truth. Socrates' "Know thyself" has as much value as the "Be virtuous" of our confessionals. They reveal a nostalgia at the same time as an ignorance. They are sterile exercises on great subjects. They are legitimate only in precisely so far as they are approximate.

And here are trees and I know their gnarled surface, water and I feel its taste. These scents of grass and stars at night, certain evenings when the heart relaxes—how shall I negate this world whose power and strength I feel? Yet all the knowledge on earth will give me nothing to assure me that this world is mine. You describe it to me and you teach me to classify it. You enumerate its laws and in my thirst for knowledge I admit that they are true. You take apart its mechanism and my hope increases. At the final stage you teach me that this wondrous and multicolored universe can be reduced to the atom and that the atom itself can be reduced to the electron. All this is good and I wait for you to continue. But you tell me of an invisible planetary system in which electrons gravitate around a nucleus. You explain this world to me with an image. I realize then that you have been reduced to poetry: I shall never know. Have I the time to become indignant? You have already changed theories. So that science that was to teach me everything ends up in a hypothesis, that lucidity founders in metaphor, that uncertainty is resolved in a work of art. What need had I of so many efforts? The soft lines of these hills and the hand of evening on this troubled heart teach me much more. I have returned to my beginning. I realize that if through science I can seize phenomena and enumerate them, I cannot, for all that, apprehend the world. Were I to trace its entire relief with my finger, I should not know any more. And you give me the choice between a description that is sure but that teaches me nothing and hypotheses that claim to teach me but that are not sure. A stranger to myself and to the world, armed solely with a thought that negates itself as soon as it asserts, what is this condition in which I can have peace only by refusing to know and to live, in which the appetite for conquest bumps into walls that defy its assaults? To will is to stir up paradoxes. Everything is ordered in such a way as to bring into being that poisoned peace produced by thoughtlessness, lack of heart, or fatal renunciations.

Hence the intelligence, too, tells me in its way that this world is absurd. Its contrary, blind reason, may well claim that all is clear; I was waiting for proof and longing for it to be right. But despite so many pretentious centuries and over the heads of so many eloquent and persuasive men, I know that is false. On this plane, at least, there is no happiness if I cannot know. That universal reason, practical or ethical, that determinism, those categories that explain everything are enough to make a decent man laugh. They have nothing to do with the mind. They negate its profound truth, which is to be enchained.

In this unintelligible and limited universe, man's fate henceforth assumes its meaning. A horde of irrationals has sprung up and surrounds him until his ultimate end. In his recovered and now studied lucidity, the feeling of the absurd becomes clear and definite. I said that the world is absurd, but I was too hasty. This world in itself is not reasonable, that is all that can be said. But what is absurd is the confrontation of this irrational and the wild longing for clarity whose call echoes in the human heart. The absurd depends as much on man as on the world. For the moment it is all that links them together. It binds them one to the other as only hatred can weld two creatures together. This is all I can discern clearly in this measureless universe where my adventure takes place. Let us pause here. If I hold to be true that absurdity that determines my relationship with life, if I become thoroughly imbued with that sentiment that seizes me in face of the world's scenes, with that lucidity imposed on me by the pursuit of a science, I must sacrifice everything to these certainties and I must see them squarely to be able to maintain them. Above all, I must adapt my behavior to them and pursue them in all their consequences. I am speaking here of decency. But I want to know beforehand if thought can live in those deserts.

The Myth of Sisyphus

The Gods had condemned Sisyphus to ceaselessly rolling a rock to the top of a mountain, whence the stone would fall back of its own weight. They had thought with some reason that there is no more dreadful punishment than futile and hopeless labor.

If one believes Homer, Sisyphus was the wisest and most prudent of mortals. According to another tradition, however, he was disposed to practice the profession of highwayman. I see no contradiction in this. Opinions differ as to the reasons why he became the futile laborer of the underworld. To begin with, he is accused of a certain levity in regard to the gods. He stole their secrets. Aegina, the daughter of Aesopus, was carried off by Jupiter. The father was shocked by that disappearance and complained to Sisyphus. He, who knew of the abduction, offered to tell about it on condition that Aesopus would give water to the citadel of Corinth. To the celestial thunderbolts he preferred the benediction of water. He was punished for this in the underworld. Homer tells us also that Sisyphus had put Death in chains. Pluto could not endure the sight of his deserted, silent empire. He dispatched the god of war, who liberated Death from the hands of her conqueror.

It is said also that Sisyphus, being near to death, rashly wanted to test his wife's love. He ordered her to cast his unburied body into the middle of the public square. Sisyphus woke up in the underworld. And there, annoyed by an obedience so contrary to human love, he obtained from Pluto permission to return to earth in order to chastise his wife. But when he had seen again the face of this world, enjoyed water and sun, warm stones and the sea, he no longer wanted to go back to the infernal darkness. Recalls, signs of anger, warnings were of no avail. Many years more he lived facing the curve of the gulf, the sparkling sea, and the smiles of earth. A decree of the gods was necessary. Mercury came and seized the impudent man by the collar and, snatching him from his joys, led him forcibly back to the underworld, where his rock was ready for him.

You have already grasped that Sisyphus is the absurd hero. He is, as much through his passions as through his torture. His scorn of the gods, his hatred of death, and his passion for life won him that unspeakable penalty in which the whole being is exerted toward accomplishing nothing. This is the price that must be paid for the passions of this earth. Nothing is told us about Sisyphus in the underworld. Myths are made for the imagination to breathe life into them. As for this myth, one sees merely the whole effort of a body straining to raise the huge stone, to roll it and push it up a slope a hundred times over; one sees the face screwed up, the cheek tight against the stone, the shoulder bracing the clay-covered mass, the foot wedging it, the fresh start with arms outstretched, the wholly human security of two earth-clotted hands. At the very end of his long effort measured by skyless space and time without depth, the purpose is achieved. Then Sisyphus watches the stone rush down in a few moments toward that lower world whence he will have to push it up again toward the summit. He goes back down to the plain.

It is during that return, that pause, that Sisyphus interests me. A face that toils so close to stones is already stone itself! I see that man going back down with a heavy yet measured step toward the torment of which he will never know the end. That hour like a breathing-space which returns as surely as his suffering, that is the hour of consciousness. At each of those moments when he leaves the heights and gradually sinks toward the lairs of the gods, he is superior to his fate. He is stronger than his rock.

If this myth is tragic, that is because its hero is conscious. Where would his torture be, indeed, if at every step the hope of succeeding upheld him? The workman of today works every day in his life at the same tasks, and this fate is no less absurd. But it is tragic only at the rare moments when it becomes conscious. Sisyphus, proletarian of the gods, powerless and rebellious, knows the whole extent of his wretched condition: it is what he thinks of during his descent. The lucidity that was to constitute his torture at the same time crowns his victory. There is no fate that cannot be surmounted by scorn.

If the descent is thus sometimes performed in sorrow, it can also take place in joy. This word is not too much. Again I fancy Sisyphus returning toward his rock, and the sorrow was in the beginning. When the images of earth cling too tightly to memory, when the call of happiness becomes too insistent, it happens that melancholy rises in man's heart: this is the rock's victory, this is the rock itself. The boundless grief is too heavy to bear. These are our nights of Gethsemane. But crushing truths perish from being acknowledged. Thus, Oedipus at the outset obeys fate without knowing it. But from the moment he knows, his tragedy begins. Yet at the same moment, blind and desperate, he realizes that the only bond linking him to the world is the cool hand of a girl. Then a tremendous remark rings out: "Despite so many ordeals, my advanced age and the nobility of my soul make me conclude that all is well." Sophocles' Oedipus, like Dostoevsky's Kirilov, thus gives the recipe for the absurd victory. Ancient wisdom confirms modern heroism.

One does not discover the absurd without being tempted to write a manual of happiness. "What! by such narrow ways—?" There is but one world, however. Happiness and the absurd are two sons of the same earth. They are inseparable. It would be a mistake to say that happiness necessarily springs from the absurd discovery. It happens as well that the feeling of the absurd springs from happiness. "I conclude that all is well," says Oedipus, and that remark is sacred. It echoes in the wild and limited universe of man. It teaches that all is not, has not been, exhausted. It drives out of this world a god who had come into it with dissatisfaction and a preference for futile sufferings. It makes of fate a human matter, which must be settled among men.

All Sisyphus' silent joy is contained therein. His fate belongs to him. His rock is his thing. Likewise, the absurd man, when he contemplates his torment, silences all the idols. In the universe suddenly restored to its silence, the myriad wondering little voices of the earth rise up.

Unconscious, secret calls, invitations from all the faces, they are the necessary reverse and price of victory. There is no sun without shadow, and it is essential to know the night. The absurd man says yes and his effort will henceforth be unceasing. If there is a personal fate, there is no higher destiny, or at least there is but one which he concludes is inevitable and despicable. For the rest, he knows himself to be the master of his days. At that subtle moment when man glances backward over his life, Sisyphus returning toward his rock, in that slight pivoting he contemplates that series of unrelated actions which becomes his fate, created by him, combined under his memory's eye and soon sealed by his death. Thus, convinced of the wholly human origin of all that is human, a blind man eager to see who knows that the night has no end, he is still on the go. The rock is still rolling.

I leave Sisyphus at the foot of the mountain! One always finds one's burden again. But Sisyphus teaches the higher fidelity that negates the gods and raises rocks. He too concludes that all is well. This universe henceforth without a master seems to him neither sterile nor futile. Each atom of that stone, each mineral flake of that nightfilled mountain, in itself forms a world. The struggle itself toward the heights is enough to fill a man's heart. One must imagine Sisyphus happy.

Nuptials

The food is bad in this café, but there is plenty of fruit, especially peaches, whose juice drips down your chin as you bite into them. Gazing avidly before me, my teeth closing on a peach, I can hear the blood pounding in my ears. The vast silence of noon hangs over the sea. Every beautiful thing has a natural pride in its own beauty, and today the world is allowing its pride to seep from every pore. Why, in its presence, should I deny the joy of living, as long as I know everything is not included in this joy? There is no shame in being happy. But today the food is king, and I call those who fear pleasure fools. They've told us so much about pride: you know, Lucifer's sin. Beware, they used to cry, you will lose your soul, and your vital powers. I have in fact learned since that a certain pride . . . But at other times I cannot prevent myself from asserting the pride in living that the whole world

From "Nuptials" in *Lyrical and Critical Essays* trans. by E. C. Kennedy (Vintage: N.Y., 1970).

conspires to give me. At Tipasa, "I see" equals "I believe," and I am not stubborn enough to deny what my hands can touch and my lips caress. I don't feel the need to make it into a work of art, but to describe it, which is different. Tipasa seems to me like a character one describes in order to give indirect expression to a certain view of the world. Like such characters, Tipasa testifies to something, and does it like a man. Tipasa is the personage I'm describing today, and it seems to me that the very act of caressing and describing my delight will insure that it has no end. There is a time for living and a time for giving expression to life. There is also a time for creating, which is less natural. For me it is enough to live with my whole body and bear witness with my whole heart. Live Tipasa, manifest its lessons, and the work of art will come later. Herein lies a freedom.

I never spent more than a day at Tipasa. A moment always comes when one has looked too long at a landscape, just as it is a long time before one sees enough of it. Mountains, the sky, the sea are like faces whose barrenness or splendor we discover by looking rather than seeing. But in order to be eloquent every face must be seen anew. One complains of growing tired too quickly, when one ought to be surprised that the work seems new only because we have forgotten it.

Toward evening I would return to a more formal section of the park, set out as a garden, just off the main road. Leaving the tumult of scents and sunlight, in the cool evening air, the mind would grow calm and the body relaxed, savoring the inner silence born of satisfied love. I would sit on a bench, watching the countryside expand with light. I was full. Above me drooped a pomegranate tree, its flower buds closed and ribbed like small tight fists containing every hope of spring. There was rosemary behind me, and I could smell only the scent of its alcohol. The hills were framed with trees, and beyond them stretched a hand of sea on which the sky, like a sail becalmed, rested in all its tenderness. I felt a strange joy in my heart, the special joy that stems from a clear conscience. There is a feeling actors have when they know they've played their part well, that is to say, when they have made their own gestures coincide with those of the ideal character they embody, having entered somehow into a prearranged design, bringing it to life with their own heartbeats. That was exactly what I felt: I had played my part well. I had performed my task as a man, and the fact that I had known joy for one entire day seemed to me not an exceptional success but the intense fulfillment of a condition which, in certain circumstances, makes it our duty to be happy. Then we are alone again, but satisfied.

Now the trees were filled with birds. The earth would give a long sigh before sliding into darkness. In a moment, with the first star, night would fall on the theater of the world. The dazzling gods of the day would return to their daily death. But other gods would come. And, though they would be darker, their ravaged faces too would come from deep within the earth.

For the moment at least, the waves' endless crashing against the shore came toward me through a space dancing with golden pollen. Sea, landscape, silence, scents of this earth, I would drink my fill of a scent-laden life, sinking my teeth into the world's fruit, golden already, overwhelmed by the feeling of its strong, sweet juice flowing on my lips. No, it was neither I nor the world that counted, but solely the harmony and silence that gave birth to the love between us. A love I was not foolish enough to claim for myself alone, proudly aware that I shared it with a whole race born in the sun and sea, alive and spirited, drawing greatness from its simplicity, and upright on the beaches, smiling in complicity at the brilliance of its skies.

9

Simone de Beauvoir,
"Woman and the Meaning of Life,"
from *The Second Sex*

Simone de Beauvoir (1908–1986) edited Les Temps Modernes *with Jean-Paul Sartre and Maurice Merleau-Ponty. The following text is from her book* The Second Sex, *the first classic of twentieth-century feminism.*

Man seeks in woman the Other as Nature and as his fellow being. But we know what ambivalent feelings Nature inspires in man. He exploits her, but she crushes him, he is born of her and dies in her; she is the source of his being and the realm that he subjugates to his will; Nature is a vein of gross material in which the soul is imprisoned, and she is the supreme reality; she is contingence and Idea, the finite and the whole; she is what opposes the Spirit, and the Spirit itself. Now ally, now enemy, she appears as the dark chaos from whence life wells up, as this life itself, and as the over-yonder toward which life tends. Woman sums up nature as Mother, Wife, and Idea; these forms now mingle and now conflict, and each of them wears a double visage.

Man has his roots deep in Nature; he has been engendered like the animals and plants; he well knows that he exists only in so far as he lives. But since the coming of the patriarchate, Life has worn in his eyes a double aspect: it is consciousness, will, transcendence, it is the spirit; and it is matter, passivity, immanence, it is the flesh. Aeschylus, Aristotle, Hippocrates proclaimed that on earth as on Olympus it is the male principle that is truly creative: from it came form, number, movement; grain grows and multiplies through Demeter's care, but the origin of the grain and its verity lie in Zeus; woman's fecundity is regarded as only a passive quality. She is the earth, and man the seed; she is Water and he is Fire. Creation has often been imagined as the marriage of fire and water; it is warmth and moisture that give rise to living things; the Sun is the husband of the Sea; the Sun, fire, are male divinities; and the Sea is one of the most nearly universal of maternal symbols. Passively the waters accept the fertilizing action of the flaming radiations. So also the sod, broken by the plowman's labor, passively receives the seeds within its furrows. But it plays a necessary part: it supports the living germ, protects it and furnishes the substance for its growth. And that is why man continued to worship the goddesses of fecundity, even after the Great Mother was dethroned;[1] he is indebted to Cybele for his crops, his herds, his whole prosperity. He even owes his own life to her. He sings the praises of water no less than fire. "Glory to the sea! Glory to its waves surrounded with sacred fire! Glory to the wave! Glory to the fire! Glory to the strange adventure," cries Goethe in the Second Part of *Faust*. Man venerates the Earth: "The matron Clay," as Blake calls her. A prophet of India advises his disciples not to spade the earth, for "it is a sin to wound or to cut, to tear the mother of us all in the labors of cultivation. . . . Shall I go take a knife and plunge it into my mother's breast? . . . Shall I hack at her flesh to reach her bones? . . . How dare I cut off my mother's hair?" In central India the Baidya also consider it a sin to "tear their earth mother's breast with the plow." Inversely, Aeschylus says of Oedipus that he "dared to seed the sacred furrow wherein he was formed." Sophocles speaks of "paternal furrows" and of the "plowman, master of a distant field that he visits only once, at the time of sowing." The loved one of an Egyptian song declares: "I am the earth!" In Islamic texts woman is called "field . . . vineyard." St. Francis of Assisi speaks in one of his hymns of "our sister, the earth, our mother, keeping and caring for us, producing all kinds of fruits, with many-colored flowers and with grass." Michelet, taking the mud baths at Acqui, exclaimed: "Dear mother of all! We are one. I came from you, to you I return! . . ." And so it is in periods when there flourishes a vitalist romanticism that desires the triumph of Life over Spirit; then the magical fertility of the land, of woman, seems to be more wonderful than the contrived operations of the male; then man dreams of losing himself anew in the maternal shadows that he may find there again the true sources of his being. The mother is the root which, sunk in

---

1. "I sing the earth, firmly founded mother of all, venerable grandmother, supporting on her soil all that lives," says a Homeric hymn. And Aeschylus also glorifies the land which "brings forth all beings, supports them, and then receives in turn their fertile seed."

the depths of the cosmos, can draw up its juices; she is the fountain whence springs forth the living water, water that is also a nourishing milk, a warm spring, a mud made of earth and water rich is restorative virtues.[2]

But more often man is in revolt against his carnal state; he sees himself as a fallen god: his curse is to be fallen from a bright and ordered heaven into the chaotic shadows of his mother's womb. This fire, this pure and active exhalation in which he likes to recognize himself, is imprisoned by woman in the mud of the earth. He would be inevitable, like a pure Idea, like the One, the All, the absolute Spirit; and he finds himself shut up in a body of limited powers, in a place and time he never chose, where he was not called for, useless, cumbersome, absurd. The contingency of all flesh is his own to suffer in his abandonment, in his unjustifiable needlessness. She also dooms him to death. This quivering jelly which is elaborated in the womb (the womb, secret and sealed like the tomb) evokes too clearly the soft viscosity of carrion for him not to turn shuddering away. Wherever life is in the making—germination, fermentation—it arouses disgust because it is made only in being destroyed; the slimy embryo begins the cycle that is completed in the putrefaction of death. Because he is horrified by needlessness and death, man feels horror at having been engendered; he would fain deny his animal ties; through the fact of his birth murderous Nature has a hold upon him.

Among primitive peoples childbirth is surrounded by the most severe taboos; in particular, the placenta must be carefully burned or thrown into the sea, for whoever should get possession of it would hold the fate of the newborn in his hands. That membranous mass by which the fetus grows is the sign of its dependency; when it is destroyed, the individual is enabled to tear himself from the living magma and become an autonomous being. The uncleanness of birth is reflected upon the mother. Leviticus and all the ancient codes impose rites of purification upon one who has given birth; and in many rural districts the ceremony of churching (blessing after childbirth) continues this tradition. We know the spontaneous embarrassment, often disguised under mocking laughter, felt by children, young girls, and men at sight of the pregnant abdomen, the swollen bosom of the woman with child. In museums

---

2. "Literally, woman is Isis, fecund nature. She is the river and the riverbed, the root and the rose, the earth and the cherry tree, the vine-stock and the grape." (Carrouges, loc. cit.)

the curious gaze at waxen embryos and preserved fetuses with the same morbid interest they show in a ravaged tomb. With all the respect thrown around it by society, the function of gestation still inspires a spontaneous feeling of revulsion. And if the little boy remains in early childhood sensually attached to the maternal flesh, when he grows older, becomes socialized, and takes note of his individual existence, this same flesh frightens him; he would ignore it and see in his mother only a moral personage. If he is anxious to believe her pure and chaste, it is less because of amorous jealousy than because of his refusal to see her as a body. The adolescent is discountenanced, he blushes, if while roaming with his companions he happens to meet his mother, his sisters, any of his female relatives: it is because their presence calls him back to those realms of immanence whence he would fly, exposes roots from which he would tear himself loose. The little boy's irritation when his mother kisses and cajoles him has the same significance; he disowns family, mother, maternal bosom. He would like to have sprung into the world, like Athena fully grown, fully armed, invulnerable. To have been conceived and then born an infant is the curse that hangs over his destiny, the impurity that contaminates his being. And, too, it is the announcement of his death. The cult of germination has always been associated with the cult of the dead. The Earth Mother engulfs the bones of her children. They are women—the Parcæ, the Moirai— who weave the destiny of mankind; but it is they, also, who cut the threads. In most popular representations Death is a woman, and it is for women to bewail the dead because death is their work.[3]

Thus the Woman-Mother has a face of shadows: she is the chaos whence all have come and whither all must one day return; she is Nothingness. In the Night are confused together the multiple aspects of the world which daylight reveals: night of spirit confined in the generality and opacity of matter, night of sleep and of nothingness. In the deeps of the sea it is night: woman is the *Mare tenebrarum*, dreaded by navigators of old; it is night in the entrails of the earth. Man is frightened of this night, the reverse of fecundity, which threatens to swallow him up. He aspires to the sky, to the light, to the sunny

---

3. Demeter typifies the *mater dolorosa*. But other goddesses—Ishtar, Artemis— are cruel. Kali holds in her hand a cranium filled with blood. A Hindu poet addresses her: "The heads of thy newly killed sons hang like a necklace about thy neck. . . . Thy form is beautiful like rain clouds, thy feet are soiled with blood."

summits, to the pure and crystalline frigidity of the blue sky; and under his feet there is a moist, warm, and darkling gulf ready to draw him down; in many a legend do we see the hero lost forever as he falls back into the maternal shadows—cave, abyss, hell.

But here again is the play of ambivalence: if germination is always associated with death, so is death with fecundity. Hated death appears as a new birth, and then it becomes blessed. The dead hero is resurrected, like Osiris, each spring, and he is regenerated by a new birth. Man's highest hope, says Jung, in *Metamorphoses of the Libido*, "is that the dark waters of death become the waters of life, that death and its cold embrace be the motherly bosom, which like the ocean, although engulfing the sun, gives birth to it again within its depths." A theme common to numerous mythologies is the burial of the sungod in the bosom of the ocean and his dazzling reappearance. And man at once wants to live but longs for repose and sleep and nothingness. He does not wish he were immortal, and so he can learn to love death. Nietzsche writes: "Inorganic matter is the maternal bosom. To be freed of life is to become true again, it is to achieve perfection. Whoever should understand that would consider it a joy to return to the unfeeling dust." Chaucer put this prayer into the mouth of an old man unable to die:

> *With my staff, night and day*
> *I strike on the ground, my mother's doorway,*
> *And I say: Ah, Mother dear, let me in.*

Man would fain affirm his individual existence and rest with pride on his "essential difference," but he wishes also to break through the barriers of the ego, to mingle with the water, the night, with Nothingness, with the Whole. Woman condemns man to finitude, but she also enables him to exceed his own limits; and hence comes the equivocal magic with which she is endued.

Myth and Reality

There are different kinds of myths. This one, the myth of woman, sublimating and immutable aspect of the human condition—namely, the "division" of humanity into two classes of individuals—is a static myth. It projects into the realm of Platonic ideas a reality that is directly experienced or is conceptualized on a basis of experience; in place of fact, value, significance, knowledge, empirical law, it substitutes a transcendental Idea, timeless, unchangeable, necessary. This idea is indisputable because it is beyond the given: it is endowed with absolute truth. Thus, as against the dispersed, contingent, and multiple existences of actual women, mythical thought opposes the Eternal Feminine, unique and changeless. If the definition provided for this concept is contradicted by the behavior of flesh-and-blood women, it is the latter who are wrong: we are told not that Femininity is a false entity, but that the women concerned are not feminine. The contrary facts of experience are impotent against the myth. In a way, however, its source is in experience. Thus it is quite true that woman is other than man, and this alterity is directly felt in desire, the embrace, love; but the real relation is one of reciprocity; as such it gives rise to authentic drama. Through eroticism, love, friendship, and their alternatives, deception, hate, rivalry, the relation is a struggle between conscious beings each of whom wishes to be essential, it is the mutual recognition of free beings who confirm one another's freedom, it is the vague transition from aversion to participation. To pose Woman is to pose the absolute Other, without reciprocity, denying against all experience that she is a subject a fellow human being.

The myth must not be confused with the recognition of significance; significance is immanent in the object; it is revealed to the mind through a living experience; whereas the myth is a transcendent Idea that escapes the mental grasp entirely. . . . There is nothing mythical in the experience that reveals the voluptuous qualities of feminine flesh, and it is not an excursion into myth if one attempts to describe them through comparisons with flowers or pebbles. But to say that Woman is Flesh, to say that the Flesh is Night and Death, or that it is the splendor of the Cosmos, is to abandon terrestrial truth and soar into an empty sky. For man also is flesh for woman; and woman is not merely a carnal object; and the flesh is clothed in special significance for each person and in each experience. And likewise it is quite true that woman—like man—is a being rooted in nature; she is more enslaved to the species than is the male, her animality is more manifest; but in her as in him the given traits are taken on through the fact of existence, she belongs to the human realm. To assimilate her to Nature is simply to act from prejudice.

10

Thomas Nagel,
"The Absurd,"
from *The Journal of Philosophy*

Thomas Nagel, Professor of Philosophy and Law at New York University, is the author of a very influential series of philosophical studies of the subjective and the objective, including his recent The View From Nowhere, The Possibility of Altruism, *and the essays collected in his* Mortal Questions.

Most people feel on occasion that life is absurd, and some feel it vividly and continually. Yet the reasons usually offered in defense of this conviction are patently inadequate: they *could* not really explain why life is absurd. Why then do they provide a natural expression for the sense that it is?

I

Consider some examples. It is often remarked that nothing we do now will matter in a million years. But if that is true, then by the same token, nothing that will be the case in a million years matters now. In particular, it does not matter now that in a million years nothing we do now will matter. Moreover, even if what we did now *were* going to matter in a million years, how could that keep our present concerns from being absurd? If their mattering now is not enough to accomplish that, how would it help if they mattered a million years from now?

Whether what we do now will matter in a million years could make the crucial difference only if its mattering in a million years depended on its mattering, period. But then to deny that whatever happens now will matter in a million years is to beg the question against its mattering, period; for in that sense one cannot know that it will not matter in a

Thomas Nagel, "The Absurd", *The Journal of Philosophy*, Vol. LXIII, No. 20 (1971).

million years whether (for example) someone now is happy or miserable, without knowing that it does not matter, period.

What we say to convey the absurdity of our lives often has to do with space or time: we are tiny specks in the infinite vastness of the universe; our lives are mere instants even on a geological time scale, let alone a cosmic one; we will all be dead any minute. But of course none of these evident facts can be what *makes* life absurd, if it is absurd. For suppose we lived forever; would not a life that is absurd if it lasts seventy years be infinitely absurd if it lasted through eternity? And if our lives are absurd given our present size, why would they be any less absurd if we filled the universe (either because we were larger or because the universe was smaller)? Reflection on our minuteness and brevity appears to be intimately connected with the sense that life is meaningless; but it is not clear what the connection is.

Another inadequate argument is that because we are going to die, all chains of justification must leave off in mid-air: one studies and works to earn money to pay for clothing, housing, entertainment, food, to sustain oneself from year to year, perhaps to support a family and pursue a career—but to what final end? All of it is an elaborate journey leading nowhere. (One will also have some effect on other people's lives, but that simply reproduces the problem, for they will die too.)

There are several replies to this argument. First, life does not consist of a sequence of activities each of which has as its purpose some later member of the sequence. Chains of justification come repeatedly to an end within life, and whether the process as a whole can be justified has no bearing on the finality of these end-points. No further justification is needed to make it reasonable to take aspirin for a headache, attend an exhibit of the work of a painter one admires, or stop a child from putting his hand on a hot stove. No larger context or further purpose is needed to prevent these acts from being pointless.

Even if someone wished to supply a further justification for pursuing all the things in life that are commonly regarded as self-justifying, that justification would have to end somewhere too. If *nothing* can justify unless it is justified in terms of something outside itself, which is also justified, then an infinite regress results, and no chain of justification can be complete. Moreover, if a finite chain of reasons cannot justify anything, what could be accomplished by an infinite chain, each link of which must be justified by something outside itself?

Since justifications must come to an end somewhere, nothing is gained by denying that they end where they appear to, within life—

or by trying to subsume the multiple, often trivial ordinary justifications of action under a single, controlling life scheme. We can be satisfied more easily than that. In fact, through its misrepresentation of the process of justification, the argument makes a vacuous demand. It insists that the reasons available within life are incomplete, but suggests thereby that all reasons that come to an end are incomplete. This makes it impossible to supply any reasons at all.

The standard arguments for absurdity appear therefore to fail as arguments. Yet I believe they attempt to express something that is difficult to state, but fundamentally correct.

II

In ordinary life a situation is absurd when it includes a conspicuous discrepancy between pretension or aspiration and reality: someone gives a complicated speech in support of a motion that has already been passed; a notorious criminal is made president of a major philanthropic foundation; you declare your love over the telephone to a recorded announcement; as you are being knighted, your pants fall down.

When a person finds himself in an absurd situation, he will usually attempt to change it, by modifying his aspirations, or by trying to bring reality into better accord with them, or by removing himself from the situation entirely. We are not always willing or able to extricate ourselves from a position whose absurdity has become clear to us. Nevertheless, it is usually possible to imagine some change that would remove the absurdity—whether or not we can or will implement it. The sense that life as a whole is absurd arises when we perceive, perhaps dimly, an inflated pretension or aspiration which is inseparable from the continuation of human life and which makes its absurdity inescapable, short of escape from life itself.

Many people's lives are absurd, temporarily or permanently, for conventional reasons having to do with their particular ambitions, circumstances, and personal relations. If there is a philosophical sense of absurdity, however, it must arise from the perception of something universal—some respect in which pretension and reality inevitably clash for us all. This condition is supplied, I shall argue, by the collision between the seriousness with which we take our lives and the perpetual possibility of regarding everything about which we are serious as arbitrary, or open to doubt.

We cannot live human lives without energy and attention, nor without making choices which show that we take some things more seriously than others. Yet we have always available a point of view outside the particular form of our lives, from which the seriousness appears gratuitous. These two inescapable viewpoints collide in us, and that is what makes life absurd. It is absurd because we ignore the doubts that we know cannot be settled, continuing to live with nearly undiminished seriousness in spite of them.

This analysis requires defense in two respects: first as regards the unavoidability of seriousness; second as regards the inescapability of doubt.

We take ourselves seriously whether we lead serious lives or not and whether we are concerned primarily with fame, pleasure, virtue, luxury, triumph, beauty, justice, knowledge, salvation, or mere survival. If we take other people seriously and devote ourselves to them, that only multiples the problem. Human life is full of effort, plans, calculation, success and failure: we *pursue* our lives, with varying degrees of sloth and energy.

It would be different if we could not step back and reflect on the process, but were merely led from impulse to impulse without selfconsciousness. But human beings do not act solely on impulse. They are prudent, they reflect, they weigh consequences, they ask whether what they are doing is worth while. Not only are their lives full of particular choices that hang together in larger activities with temporal structure: they also decide in the broadest terms what to pursue and what to avoid, what the priorities among their various aims should be, and what kind of people they want to be or become. Some men are faced with such choices by the large decisions they make from time to time; some merely by reflection on the course their lives are taking as the product of countless small decisions. They decide whom to marry, what profession to follow, whether to join the Country Club, or the Resistance; or they may just wonder why they go on being salesmen or academics or taxi drivers, and then stop thinking about it after a certain period of inconclusive reflection.

Although they may be motivated from act to act by those immediate needs with which life presents them, they allow the process to continue by adhering to the general system of habits and the form of life in which such motives have their place—or perhaps only by clinging to life itself. They spend enormous quantities of energy, risk, and calculation on the details. Think of how an ordinary individual sweats over his appearance, his health, his sex life, his emotional honesty, his social utility, his self-knowledge, the quality of his ties with family; colleagues, and friends, how well he does his job, whether he understands the world and what is going on in it. Leading a human life is a full-time occupation, to which everyone devotes decades of intense concern.

This fact is so obvious that it is hard to find it extraordinary and important. Each of us lives his own life—lives with himself twenty-four hours a day. What else is he supposed to do—live someone else's life? Yet humans have the special capacity to step back and survey themselves, and the lives to which they are committed, with that detached amazement which comes from watching an ant struggle up a heap of sand. Without developing the illusion that they are able to escape from their highly specific and idiosyncratic position, they can view it *sub specie aeternitatis*—and the view is at once sobering and comical.

The crucial backward step is not taken by asking for still another justification in the chain, and failing to get it. The objections to that line of attack have already been stated; justifications come to an end. But this is precisely what provides universal doubt with its object. We step back to find that the whole system of justification and criticism, which controls our choices and supports our claims to rationality, rests on responses and habits that we never question, that we should not know how to defend without circularity, and to which we shall continue to adhere even after they are called into question.

The things we do or want without reasons, and without requiring reasons—the things that define what is a reason for us and what is not—are the starting points of our skepticism. We see ourselves from outside, and all the contingency and specificity of our aims and pursuits become clear. Yet when we take this view and recognize what we do as arbitrary, it does not disengage us from life, and there lies our absurdity: not in the fact that such an external view can be taken of us, but in the fact that we ourselves can take it, without ceasing to be the person whose ultimate concerns are so coolly regarded.

III

One may try to escape the position by seeking broader ultimate concerns, from which it is impossible to step back—the idea being that absurdity results because what we take seriously is something small and insignificant and individual. Those seeking to supply their lives with meaning usually envision a role or function in something larger than themselves. They therefore seek fulfillment in service to society, the state, the revolution, the progress of history, the advance of science, or religion and the glory of God.

But a role in some larger enterprise cannot confer significance unless that enterprise is itself significant. And its significance must come back to what we can understand, or it will not even appear to give us what we are seeking. If we learned that we were being raised to provide food for other creatures fond of human flesh, who planned to turn us into cutlets before we got too stringy—even if we learned that the human race had been developed by animal breeders precisely for this purpose—that would still not give our lives meaning, for two reasons. First, we would still be in the dark as to the significance of the lives of those other beings; second, although we might acknowledge that this culinary role would make our lives meaningful to them, it is not clear how it would make them meaningful to us.

Admittedly, the usual form of service to a higher being is different from this. One is supposed to behold and partake of the glory of God, for example, in a way in which chickens do not share in the glory of coq au vin. The same is true of service to a state, a movement, or a revolution. People can come to feel, when they are part of something bigger, that it is part of them too. They worry less about what is peculiar to themselves, but identify enough with the larger enterprise to find their role in it fulfilling.

However, any such larger purpose can be put in doubt in the same way that the aims of an individual life can be, and for the same reasons. It is as legitimate to find ultimate justification there as to find it earlier, among the details of individual life. But this does not alter the fact that justifications come to an end when we are content to have them end—when we do not find it necessary to look any further. If we can step back from the purposes of individual life and doubt their point, we can step back also from the progress of human history, or of science, or the success of a society, or the kingdom, power, and glory of God,[1] and put all these things into question in the same way. What seems to us to confer meaning, justification, significance, does so in virtue of the fact that we need no more reasons after a certain point.

What makes doubt inescapable with regard to the limited aims of individual life also makes it inescapable with regard to any larger

1. Cf. Robert Nozick, "Teleology," *Mosaic*, xii, 1 (Spring 1971): 27/8.

purpose that encourages the sense that life is meaningful. Once the fundamental doubt has begun, it cannot be laid to rest.

Camus maintains in *The Myth of Sisyphus* that the absurd arises because the world fails to meet our demands for meaning. This suggests that the world might satisfy those demands if it were different. But now we can see that this is not the case. There does not appear to be any conceivable world (containing us) about which unsettlable doubts could not arise. Consequently the absurdity of our situation derives not from a collision between our expectations and the world, but from a collision within ourselves.

IV

It may be objected that the standpoint from which these doubts are supposed to be felt does not exist—that if we take the recommended backward step we will land on thin air, without any basis for judgment about the natural responses we are supposed to be surveying. If we retain our usual standards of what is important, then questions about the significance of what we are doing with our lives will be answerable in the usual way. But if we do not, then those questions can mean nothing to us, since there is no longer any content to the idea of what matters, and hence no content to the idea that nothing does.

But this objection misconceives the nature of the backward step. It is not supposed to give us an understanding of what is *really* important, so that we see by contrast that our lives are insignificant. We never, in the course of these reflections, abandon the ordinary standards that guide our lives. We merely observe them in operation, and recognize that if they are called into question we can justify them only by reference to themselves, uselessly. We adhere to them because of the way we are put together; what seems to us important or serious or valuable would not seem so if we were differently constituted.

In ordinary life, to be sure, we do not judge a situation absurd unless we have in mind some standards of seriousness, significance, or harmony with which the absurd can be contrasted. This contrast is not implied by the philosophical judgment of absurdity, and that might be thought to make the concept unsuitable for the expression of such judgments. This is not so, however, for the philosophical judgment depends on another contrast which makes it a natural extension from more ordinary cases. It departs from them only in contrasting the pretensions of life with a larger context in which *no* standards can be discovered, rather than with a context from which alternative, overriding standards may be applied.

V

In this respect, as in others, philosophical perception of the absurd resembles epistemological skepticism. In both cases the final, philosophical doubt is not contrasted with any unchallenged certainties, though it is arrived at by extrapolation from examples of doubt within the system of evidence or justification, where a contrast with other certainties is implied. In both cases our limitedness joins with a capacity to transcend those limitations in thought (thus seeing them as limitations, and as inescapable).

Skepticism begins when we include ourselves in the world about which we claim knowledge. We notice that certain types of evidence convince us, that we are content to allow justifications of belief to come to an end at certain points, that we feel we know many things even without knowing or having grounds for believing the denial of others which, if true, would make what we claim to know false.

For example, I know that I am looking at a piece of paper, although I have no adequate grounds to claim I know that I am not dreaming; and if I am dreaming then I am not looking at a piece of paper. Here an ordinary conception of how appearance may diverge from reality is employed to show that we take our world largely for granted; the certainty that we are not dreaming cannot be justified except circularly, in terms of those very appearances which are being put in doubt. It is somewhat farfetched to suggest I may be dreaming; but the possibility is only illustrative. It reveals that our claim to knowledge depend on our not feeling it necessary to exclude certain incompatible alternatives, and the dreaming possibility or the total-hallucination possibility are just representatives for limitless possibilities most of which we cannot even conceive.[2]

Once we have taken the backward step to an abstract view of our whole system of beliefs, evidence, and justification, and seen that it works only, despite its pretensions, by taking the world largely for

---

2. I am aware that skepticism about the external world is widely thought to have been refuted, but I have remained convinced of its irrefutability since being exposed at Berkeley to Thompson Clarke's largely unpublished ideas on the subject.

granted, we are *not* in a position to contrast all these appearances with an alternative reality. We cannot shed our ordinary responses, and if we could it would leave us with no means of conceiving a reality of any kind.

It is the same in the practical domain. We do not step outside our lives to a new vantage point from which we see what is really, objectively significant. We continue to take life largely for granted while seeing that all our decisions and certainties are possible only because there is a great deal we do not bother to rule out.

Both epistemological skepticism and a sense of the absurd can be reached via initial doubts posed within systems of evidence and justification that we accept, and can be stated without violence to our ordinary concepts. We can ask not only why we should believe there is a floor under us, but also why we should believe the evidence of our senses at all—and at some point the framable questions will have outlasted the answers. Similarly, we can ask not only why we should take aspirin, but why we should take trouble over our own comfort at all. The fact that we shall take the aspirin without waiting for an answer to this last question does not show that it is an unreal question. We shall also continue to believe there is a floor under us without waiting for an answer to the other question. In both cases it is this unsupported natural confidence that generates skeptical doubts; so it cannot be used to settle them.

Philosophical skepticism does not cause us to abandon our ordinary beliefs, but it lends them a peculiar flavor. After acknowledging that their truth is incompatible with possibilities that we have no grounds for believing do not obtain—apart from grounds in those very beliefs which we have called into question—we return to our familiar convictions with a certain irony and resignation. Unable to abandon the natural responses on which they depend, we take them back, like a spouse who has run off with someone else and then decided to return; but we regard them differently (not that the new attitude is necessarily inferior to the old, in either case).

The same situation obtains after we have put in question the seriousness with which we take our lives and human life in general and have looked at ourselves without presuppositions. We then return to our lives, as we must, but our seriousness is laced with irony. Not that irony enables us to escape the absurd. It is useless to mutter: "Life is meaningless; life is meaningless . . ." as an accompaniment to everything we do. In continuing to live and work and strive, we take ourselves seriously in action no matter what we say.

What sustains us, in belief as in action, is not reason or justification, but something more basic than these—for we go on in the same way even after we are convinced that the reasons have given out.[3] If we tried to rely entirely on reason, and pressed it hard, our lives and beliefs would collapse—a form of madness that may actually occur if the inertial force of taking the world and life for granted is somehow lost. If we lose our grip on that, reason will not give it back to us.

VI

In viewing ourselves from a perspective broader than we can occupy in the flesh, we become spectators of our own lives. We cannot do very much as pure spectators of our own lives, so we continue to lead them, and devote ourselves to what we are able at the same time to view as no more than a curiosity, like the ritual of an alien religion.

This explains why the sense of absurdity finds its natural expression in those bad arguments with which the discussion began. Reference to our small size and short lifespan and to the fact that all of mankind will eventually vanish without a trace are metaphors for the backward step which permits us to regard ourselves from without and to find the particular form of our lives curious and slightly surprising. By feigning a nebula's-eye view, we illustrate the capacity to see ourselves without presuppositions, as arbitrary, idiosyncratic, highly specific occupants of the world, one of countless possible forms of life.

Before turning to the question whether the absurdity of our lives is something to be regretted and if possible escaped, let me consider what would have to be given up in order to avoid it.

3. As Hume says in a famous passage of the *Treatise:* "Most fortunately it happens, that since reason is incapable of dispelling these clouds, nature herself suffices to that purpose, and cures me of this philosophical melancholy and delirium, either by relaxing this bent of mind, or by some avocation, and lively impression of my senses, which obliterates all these chimeras. I dine, I play a game of backgammon, I converse, and am merry with my friends; and when after three or four hours' amusement, I would return to these speculations, they appear so cold and strain'd, and ridiculous, that I cannot find in my heart to enter into them any farther" (Book 1, Part, 4, Section 7; Selby-Bigge, p. 269).

Why is the life of a mouse not absurd? The orbit of the moon is not absurd either, but that involves no strivings or aims at all. A mouse, however, has to work to stay alive. Yet he is not absurd, because he lacks the capacities for self-consciousness and self-transcendence that would enable him to see that he is only a mouse. It that *did* happen, his life would become absurd, since self-awareness would not make him cease to be a mouse and would not enable him to rise above his mousely strivings. Bringing his new-found self-consciousness with him, he would have to return to his meager yet frantic life, full of doubts that he was unable to answer, but also full of purpose that he was unable to abandon.

Given that the transcendental step is natural to us humans, can we avoid absurdity by refusing to take that step and remaining entirely within our sublunar lives? Well, we cannot refuse consciously, for to do that we would have to be aware of the viewpoint we were refusing to adopt. The only way to avoid the relevant self-consciousness would be either never to attain it or to forget it—neither of which can be achieved by the will.

On the other hand, it is possible to expend effort on an attempt to destroy the other component of the absurd—abandoning one's earthly, individual, human life in order to identify as completely as possible with that universal viewpoint from which human life seems arbitrary and trivial. (This appears to be the ideal of certain Oriental religions.) If one succeeds, then one will not have to drag the superior awareness through a strenuous mundane life, and absurdity will be diminished.

However, insofar as this self-etiolation is the result of effort, will-power, asceticism, and so forth, it requires that one take oneself seriously as an individual—that one be willing to take considerable trouble to avoid being creaturely and absurd. Thus one may undermine the aim of unworldliness by pursuing it too vigorously. Still, if someone simply allowed his individual, animal nature to drift and respond to impulse, without making the pursuit of its needs a central conscious aim, then he might, at considerable dissociative cost, achieve a life that was less absurd than most. It would not be a meaningful life either, of course; but it would not involve the engagement of a transcendent awareness in the assiduous pursuit of mundane goals. And that is the main condition of absurdity—the dragooning of an unconvinced transcendent consciousness into the service of an immanent, limited enterprise like a human life.

VII

The final escape is suicide; but before adopting any hasty solutions, it would be wise to consider carefully whether the absurdity of our existence truly presents us with a *problem*, to which some solution must be found—a way of dealing with prima facie disaster. That is certainly the attitude with which Camus approaches the issue, and it gains support from the fact that we are all eager to escape from absurd situations on a smaller scale.

Camus—not on uniformly good grounds—rejects suicide and the other solutions he regards as escapist. What he recommends is defiance or scorn. We can salvage our dignity, he appears to believe, by shaking a fist at the world which is deaf to our pleas, and continuing to live in spite of it. This will not make our lives un-absurd, but it will lend them a certain nobility.[4]

This seems to me romantic and slightly self-pitying. Our absurdity warrants neither that much distress nor that much defiance. At the risk of falling into romanticism by a different route, I would argue that absurdity is one of the most human things about us: a manifestation of our most advanced and interesting characteristics. Like skepticism in epistemology, it is possible only because we possess a certain kind of insight—the capacity to transcend ourselves in thought.

If a sense of the absurd is a way of perceiving our true situation (even though the situation is not absurd until the perception arises), then what reason can we have to resent or escape it? Like the capacity for epistemological skepticism, it results from the ability to understand our human limitations. It need not be a matter for agony unless we make it so. Nor need it evoke a defiant contempt of fate that allows us to feel brave or proud. Such dramatics, even if carried on in private, betray a failure to appreciate the cosmic unimportance of the situation. If *sub specie aeternitatis* there is no reason to believe that anything matters, then that doesn't matter either, and we can approach our absurd lives with irony instead of heroism or despair.

---

4. "Sisyphus, proletarian of the gods, powerless and rebellious, knows the whole extent of his wretched condition: it is what he thinks of during his descent. The lucidity that was to constitute his torture at the same time crowns his victory. There is no fate that cannot be surmounted by scorn" (*The Myth of Sisyphus*, Vintage edition, p. 90).

11

Jonathan Westphal and Christopher Cherry,
"Is Life Absurd?"
from *Philosophy*

Christopher Cherry is the Master of Eliot College in the University of Kent, in Canterbury, England. He has written extensively in the areas of philosophy of mind, philosophy of religion and literature, and ethics.

Jonathan Westphal, who teaches philosophy at Idaho State University, is the author of Colour: A Philosophical Introduction *and* Philosophical Propositions.

I

Thomas Nagel believes, with some existentialists, that life is absurd.[1] We shall criticize his belief, as well as the anodyne he offers.

By an absurd situation Nagel means one which includes 'a conspicuous discrepancy between pretension and aspiration and reality'. He gives examples: '...you declare your love over the telephone to a recorded announcement; as you are being knighted your pants fall down'.[2] So Nagel's use of 'absurd' is quite a bit stronger than the ordinary English one, in which it is merely something incongruous, ridiculous or silly, and does not include the contrast between pretension and reality. Nagel believes that human life is bound to be absurd in his sense. We are bound, on the one hand, to commitment or 'pretension' about what we do in life. We value our plans and projects in certain ways, and in this sense we must be serious about living our lives. Life lived within our valuations is lived from what Nagel calls an 'internal perspective'. On the other hand, beings such as we are prone to reflection about our lives. Nagel does not show anywhere why this is any more than a simple failure of nerve. Why should we take

"Is Life Absurd?" from *Philosophy* (1990), with permission by Cambridge University Press.

1. 'The Absurd', Selection 10 in this volume, p. 86.
2. Ibid., p. 88.

up someone *else's* point of view? Nor does he tell us much about the
nature of the internal perspective. This must be inferred from what
he says about the external perspective, which is according to him the
expression of a certain sort of skepticism characteristic of conscious
beings who can take the backward step of self-reflection. He character-
izes the external perspective in a series of metaphors. We see ourselves
and our lives 'with cool regard', from a 'nebula's eye point of view',
or we exercise the capacity to see ourselves 'without presuppositions'
(what does this have to do with nebulae?) We see ourselves 'from the
outside', presumably minus our hopes and wishes, our values and
interpretations of things, as 'spectators of our own lives', '*sub specie
aeternitatis*', and take a view of life similar to the 'detached amazement
which comes from watching an ant struggle up a heap of sand'.

We propose to defend the value of certain activities in life by drawing
attention to one kind of 'pretension' which is immune to the value
doubt. This is not to deny that there are ways of living and types of
value which are vulnerable. Examples are those which are neurotically
thought out, certain political values, and inauthentic ones. We return
to this in IV.

II

Consider someone who is serious about a life devoted to music.
This is partly for him not to entertain the thought, or not to be able
to entertain it, that music might ultimately be insignificant, as compared,
perhaps, with cosmic noise, or that it has no particular significance in
the scheme of the physical universe. It is for him to be absorbed in
music. His absorption destroys the skeptical or external perspective,
and renders it flimsy, or meaningless, or absurd. We cannot seriously
attend to a piece of music, say the heart-breaking Adagio in F Sharp
Minor of Mozart's Twenty-Third Piano Concerto, and, at the same
time, declare it to be ultimately pointless. The Concerto cannot be
adequately described, even in a fairly thin or rudimentary way, without
disabling the external perspective. To describe it minus its so-called
'emotional value' is in fact not to underdescribe it or to describe it in
a minimal sort of way, but to *misdescribe* it. Are the words 'harmony',
'chord', 'discord', 'minor key', 'resolution', factual or evaluative? (A
harmony is (O.E.D.) 'the combination of musical notes so as to produce
a pleasing effect'.) Are these words proper to a description of sound

from the external point of view or to one from an internal point of view?

III

These points are not peculiar to a life devoted to music. If we contemplate the life of any very gifted man who is also what might be called a man of integrity or humanity, we may find in it *nothing* on which images of gratuitousness and meaninglessness, or doubt, can get a purchase. We are imagining that this life is lived with such grace and inner resourcefulness that it outshines the obscure arguments to the effect that everything must ultimately be destroyed, or that nothing, in itself, matters, or the reflective consciousness which, according to Nagel, stands behind them. Such a life would be lived without pretension, in the sense that no formal claims about Value are made for it, so that there are none for the external perspective to negate, and in the sense that it is in a certain way unostentatious, not puffed up, true or fine, lived without illusion or pretence. Chagall writes at the end of *My Life:*[3]

> These pages have the same meaning as a painted surface. If there were a hiding place in my pictures, I would slip them into it . . . Or perhaps they would stick to the back of one of my characters or maybe on to the trousers of the 'Musician' in my mural . . .

Where could the pretension be in that? It is playful, certainly, but not unserious. What could it mean? Chagall's View of Life? From the skeptical or external point of view, it is hard to imagine. But then this is a perspective deprived of life and art, which must view life as arbitrary and art as artifice and deception.

For pretension and aspiration to become vulnerable to the external perspective, they must be conceived in their least subtle and imaginative forms. This is notoriously easy to do for political and social aspirations and values. The external perspective gains its power when imagination—the imagination used in thinking about music, or painting, or one's life—is at its lowest ebb. It is characteristic of the most significant aspirations that they are very complex and difficult to state. *That* is why they cannot be incorporated into the external perspective of a soulless vast physical universe. For this is as optional a view as any other, and has in it more than an element of caricature.

3. Marc Chagall, *My Life,* London: Peter Owen, 1985, 171.

IV

Nagel says that we may try to escape absurdity by seeking broader ultimate concerns, from which it is impossible to step back,[4] concerns which are larger than oneself, such as 'service to society, the state, the revolution, the progress of history, the advance of science, or religion and the glory of God'.[5] Some of these concerns are sillier than others, or one is. But they are all liable to just the same sort of external doubt. We can see service to history, the state, the revolution, etc., from the skeptical point of view, and there is no gain. This may be because the commitments are clumsily or unintelligently thought out. We become international communists and traitors because we are cross with the British Empire for disappearing and leaving us nothing of a suitable size to rule. Or we study philosophy, as a very distinguished philosopher has told us he did, because we wish to be seen walking about with a copy of Plato's *Republic* in our back pockets. These types of inauthenticity are especially vulnerable to the external perspective, to someone who sees us, not from as far away as a nebula, but with a 'cool regard' from just over the road.

The concerns of art, science and religion are different from this in certain important respects. Chagall's concerns, as these are described in *My Life*, were not wider or more confused than everyday concerns, but actually narrower and even more focused. Religion and science also introduce more of a certain sort of meaning into life or a life. This happens, however, not when the smaller individual life is located within some huger scheme, but the other way round. The sense of the 'larger' enterprise is determined by the way in which it contributes to the lives of individuals. The two are in any case inseparable.

One thinks of Nabokov's obsession with just one group of butterflies, or Tycho Brahe's patient recording over twenty years of the movements of the planets. Or consider what the young Gilbert Ryle wrote about religion and faith in a letter to J. King Gordon (25 October 1924):[6]

I was cynical & skeptical & shall I say *clever* before I knew you all: now I hate cynicism and though I have not in the ordinary sense of the words *a* religion or *a* faith: yet I understand what the former is & I know that the

4. Nagel, p. 90.
5. Ibid.
6. J. King Gordon, 'Gilbert Ryle: the beginnings of wisdom', copy of ms. in the Philosophy Sub-faculty Library, 14 Merton Street, Oxford, 14.

latter is something which holds life together & makes it true & is not itself
a mere collection of accepted dogmas & beliefs but is a real or the real
thing in life that is not just surface . . .

'Something which holds life together and makes it true' is not a larger
context or concern, but, in a sense familiar from writings of mystical
religion, a smaller and more personal one. This sort of point does not
apply to service to the state, the revolution or the progress of history.
But that is also a characteristic problem for these ideals.

V

No better than Nagel's argument for absurdity is his proposed anti-
dote to it. He prescribes *irony* for the absurdity of life, rather than for
example the scorn of Camus. 'If *sub specie aeternitatis* there is no reason
to believe that anything matters, then that does not matter either, and
we can approach our absurd lives with irony instead of heroism and
despair'.[7] But this recursive intuition (that if nothing matters then
that does not matter) is not really solidly convincing. Perhaps nothing
matters *except* that nothing matters. Why not? Nor is it at all clear why
irony is the overall best response to absurdity. An ironic attitude towards
our allegedly absurd situation is perhaps a New York response to the
problem, certainly an urban one, and many people would be unable
to adopt it, due to temperament, or education and upbringing. What
is to be said to them?[8]
It makes much more sense to *ignore* the problem and the external
perspective, and if we are unable to dismiss them intellectually, to dine,
play backgammon and make merry with our friends: Hume's remedy for
too much metaphysics. The same result can be achieved by occupying
ourselves with interesting work. These irenic strategies towards the
alleged ultimate disvalue are sensible, not because they blot out the
problem, but because the problem is wrongly set, and real life can
restore our intuition that this is so. Life really does not call for scorn or
despair, and these large attitudes are, as Nagel himself notes, misplaced.
Camus' scorn, he says is, 'romantic and slightly self-pitying'.[9] This is
bad, of course. But why is irony any better? Because it is more refined?

7. Nagel, op. cit., p. 97.
8. Ibid., pp. 93–95.
9. Ibid., p. 97.

What is wrong here is not some feature of whatever attitude one takes to life, but the whole idea that it calls for one defiant last-ditch defence. This is the romantic idea, common to existentialism, certain Christian theologies, and the heroic materialism of the last century. For example, 'Brief and powerless is man's life: on him and all his race the slow sure doom falls pitiless and dark. Blind to good and evil, reckless of destruction, omnipotent matter rolls on its relentless way . . . "[10] To avoid this cosmic version of the external perspective, all we have to do is to recognize it for the colourful rubbish it is.

10. Bertrand Russell, 'A Free Man's Worship', reprinted in E. D. Klemke, *The Meaning of Life*, Oxford, 1981, 61.

12

Richard Hare,
"Nothing Matters,"
from *Applications of Moral Philosophy*

Richard Hare, until 1963 White's Professor of Moral Philosophy at the University of Oxford, produced in The Language of Morals, *and* Freedom and Reason, *the most widely respected and discussed writings on ethics of the 1950s and 1960s.*

I

I want to start by telling you a story about something which once happened in my house in Oxford—I cannot remember now all the exact details, but will do my best to be accurate. It was about nine years ago, and we had staying with us a Swiss boy from Lausanne; he was about 18 years old and had just left school. He came of a Protestant family and was both sincerely religious and full of the best ideals. My wife and I do not read French very well, and so we had few French books in the house; but those we had we put by his bedside; they included one or two anthologies of French poetry, the works of Villon, the confessions of Rousseau and, lastly, *L'Etranger* by Camus. After our friend had been with us for about a week, and we thought we were getting to know him as a cheerful, vigourous, enthusiastic young man of a sort that anybody is glad to know, he surprised us one morning by asking for cigarettes—he had not smoked at all up till then—and retiring to his room, where he smoked them one after the other, coming down hurriedly to meals, during which he would say nothing at all. After dinner in the evening, at which he ate little, he said he would go for a walk. So he went out and spent the next three hours—as we learnt from him later—tramping round and round Port Meadow (which is an enormous, rather damp field beside the river Thames on the

R. M. Hare, "Nothing Matters", in R. M. Hare, *Applications of Moral Philosophy*, London, Macmillan, 1972.

outskirts of Oxford). Since we were by this time rather worried about
what could be on his mind, when he came back at about eleven o'clock
we sat him down in an armchair and asked him what the trouble was.
It appeared that he had been reading Camus's novel, and had become
convinced that *nothing matters*. I do not remember the novel very well;
but at the end of it, I think, the hero, who is about to be executed for
a murder in which he saw no particular point even when he committed
it, shouts, with intense conviction, to the priest who is trying to get
him to confess and receive absolution, "Nothing matters." It was this
proposition of the truth of which our friend had become convinced:
Rien, rien n'avait d'importance.

Now this was to me in many ways an extraordinary experience. I
have known a great many students at Oxford, and not only have I never
known one of them affected in this way, but when I have told this story
to English people they have thought that I was exaggerating, or that
our Swiss friend must have been an abnormal, peculiar sort of person.
Yet he was not; he was about as well-balanced a young man as you
could find. There was, however, no doubt at all about the violence
with which he had been affected by what he had read. And as he sat
there, it occurred to me that as a moral philosopher I ought to have
something to say to him that would be relevant to his situation.

Now in Oxford, moral philosophy is thought of primarily as the
study of the concepts and the language that we use when we are
discussing moral questions: we are concerned with such problems as
"What does it mean to say that something *matters*, or *does not matter?*"
We are often accused of occupying ourselves with trivial questions
about words; but this sort of question is not really trivial; if it were,
philosophy itself would be a trivial subject. For philosophy as we know
it began when Socrates refused to answer questions about, for example,
what *was* right or wrong before he had discussed the question "*What
is it to be* right or wrong?"; and it does not really make any difference
if this question is put in the form "What is rightness?" or "What is
the meaning of the word 'right'?" or "What is its use in our language?"
So, like Socrates, I thought that the correct way to start my discussion
with my Swiss friend was to ask what was the meaning or function of
the word "matters" in our language; what is it to be important?

He very soon agreed that when we say something matters or is
important what we are doing, in saying this, is to express concern about
that something. If a person is concerned about something and wishes
to give expression in language to this concern, two ways of doing this

are to say "This is important" or "It matters very much that so and so should happen and not so and so." Here, however, I must utter a warning lest I be misunderstood. The word "express" has been used recently as a technical term by a certain school of moral philosophers known as the Emotivists. The idea has therefore gained currency that if a philosopher says that a certain form of expression is used to *express* something, there must be something a bit shady or suspicious about that form of expression. I am not an emotivist, and I am using the word "express" as it is normally used outside philosophical circles, in a perfectly neutral sense. When I say that the words "matters" and "important" are used to express concern, I am no more committed to an emotivist view of the meaning of those words than I would be if I said "The word 'not' is used in English to express negation" or "Mathematicians use the symbol '+' to express the operation of addition."

Having secured my friend's agreement on this point, I then pointed out to him something that followed immediately from it. This is that when somebody says that something matters or does not matter, we want to know *whose* concern is being expressed or otherwise referred to. If the function of the expression "matters" is to express concern, and if concern is always *somebody's* concern, we can always ask, when it is said that something matters or does not matter, "Whose concern?" The answer to these questions is in most cases obvious from the context. In the simplest cases it is the speaker who is expressing his own concern. If we did not know what it meant in these simple cases to say that something matters, we should not be able to understand what is meant by more complicated, indirect uses of the expression. We know what it is to be concerned about something and to express this concern by saying that it matters. So we understand when anybody else says the same thing: he is then expressing his own concern. But sometimes we say things like "It matters (or doesn't matter) to *him* whether so and so happens." Here we are not expressing our own concern; we are referring indirectly to the concern of the person about whom we are speaking. In such cases, in contrast to the more simple cases, it is usual to give a clear indication of the person whose concern is being referred to. Thus we say, "It doesn't matter to him." If we said "It doesn't matter," and left out the words "to him," it could be assumed in ordinary speech, in the absence of any indication to the contrary, that the speaker was expressing his *own* unconcern.

II

With these explanations made, my friend and I then returned to the remark at the end of Camus's novel, and asked whether we really understood it. "Nothing matters" is printed on the page. So somebody's unconcern for absolutely everything is presumably being expressed or referred to. But whose? As soon as we ask this question we see that there is something funny, not indeed about the remark as made by the character in the novel, in the context in which he is described as making it (though there is something funny even about that, as we shall see), but about the effect of this remark upon my friend. If we ask whose unconcern is being expressed, there are three people to be considered, one imaginary and two real: the character in the novel, the writer of the novel, and its reader, my Swiss friend. The idea that Camus was expressing his *own* unconcern about everything can be quickly dismissed. For to produce a work of art as good as this novel is something which cannot be done by someone who is not most deeply concerned, not only with the form of the work, but with its content. It is quite obvious that it mattered very much to Camus to say as clearly and tellingly as possible what he had to say; and this argues a concern not only for the work, but for its readers.

As for the character in the novel, who thus expresses his unconcern, a writer of a novel can put what sentiments he pleases in the mouths of his characters—subject to the limits of verisimilitude. By the time we have read this particular novel, it seems to us not inappropriate that the character who is the hero of it should express unconcern about absolutely everything. In fact, it has been pretty clear right from the beginning of the novel that he has not for a long time been deeply concerned about anything; that is the sort of person he is. And indeed there are such people. I do not mean to say that there has ever been anybody who has literally been concerned about *nothing*. For what we are concerned about comes out in what we choose to *do;* to be concerned about something is to be disposed to make certain choices, certain efforts, in the attempt to affect in some way that about which we are concerned. I do not think that anybody has ever been *completely* unconcerned about *everything*, because everybody is always doing something, choosing one thing rather than another; and these choices reveal what it is he thinks matters, even if he is not able to express this in words. And the character in Camus's novel, though throughout the book he is depicted as a person who is rather given to unconcern, is depicted at the end of it, when he says these words, as one who is spurred by something—it is not clear what: a sense of conviction, or revelation, or merely irritation—to seize the priest by the collar of his cassock with such violence, while saying this to him, that they had to be separated by the warders. There is something of a contradiction in being so violently concerned to express unconcern; if nothing *really* mattered to him, one feels, he would have been too bored to make this rather dramatic scene.

Still, one must allow writers to portray their characters as their art seems to require, with all their inconsistencies. But why, because an imaginary Algerian prisoner expressed unconcern for the world which he was shortly to leave, should my friend, a young Swiss student with the world before him, come to share the same sentiments? I therefore asked him whether it was really true that nothing mattered to him. And of course it was not true. He was not in the position of the prisoner but in the position of most of us; he was concerned not about nothing, but about many things. His problem was not to find something to be concerned about—something that mattered—but to reduce to some sort of order those things that were matters of concern to him; to decide which mattered most; which he thought worth pursuing even at the expense of some of the others—in short, to decide what he really wanted.

III

The values of most of us come from two main sources; our own wants and our imitation of other people. If it be true that to imitate other people is, especially in the young, one of the strongest desires, these two sources of our values can be seen to have a common head. What is so difficult about growing up is the integration into one stream of these two kinds of values. In the end, if we are to be able sincerely to say that something matters for us, we must ourselves be concerned about it; other people's concern is not enough, however much in general we may want to be like them. Thus, to take an aesthetic example, my parents may like the music of Bach, and I may want to be like my parents; but this does not mean that I can say sincerely that I like the music of Bach. What often happens in such cases is that I *pretend* to like Bach's music; this is of course in fact *mauvaise foi*—hypocrisy; but none the less it is quite often by this means that I come in the end to like the music. Pretending to like something, if one does it in the right spirit, is one of the best ways of getting really to like it. It is in this way that nearly all of us get to like alcohol. Most developed art is so complex and remote from what people like at the first experience, that it would be altogether impossible for new generations to get to enjoy the developed art of their time, or even that of earlier generations, without at least some initial dishonesty.

Nevertheless, we also often rebel against the values of our elders. A young man may say, "My parents think it matters enormously to go to church every Sunday; but I can't feel at all concerned about it." Or he may say, "Most of the older generation think it a disgrace not to fight for one's country in time of war; but isn't it more of a disgrace not to make a stand against the whole murderous business by becoming a pacifist?" It is by reactions such as these that people's values get altered from generation to generation.

Now to return to my Swiss friend. I had by this time convinced him that many things did matter for him, and that the expression "Nothing matters" in his mouth could only be (if he understood it) a piece of playacting. Of course he didn't actually understand it. It is very easy to assume that all words works in the same way; to show the differences is one of the chief ways in which philosophers can be of service to mankind. My friend had not understood that the function of the word "matters" is to express concern; he had thought mattering was something (some activity or process) that things did, rather like chattering; as if the sentence "My wife matters to me" were similar in logical function to the sentence "My wife chatters to me." If one thinks that, one may begin to wonder what this activity is, called mattering; and one may begin to observe the world closely (aided perhaps by the clear cold descriptions of a novel like that of Camus) to see if one can catch anything doing something that could be called mattering; and when we can observe nothing going on which seems to correspond to this name, it is easy for the novelist to persuade us that after all *nothing matters*. To which the answer is, " 'Matters' isn't that sort of word; it isn't intended to *describe* something that things do, but to express our concern about what they do; so of course we can't observe things mattering; but that doesn't mean that they don't matter (as we can be readily assured if, as I told my friend to do, we follow Hume's advice and 'turn our reflexion into our own breast'[1])."

1. *Treatise*, III 1 i.

There are real struggles and perplexities about what matters most; but alleged worries about whether anything matters at all are in most cases best dispelled by Hume's other well-known remedy for similar doubts about the possibility of causal reasoning—a good game of backgammon.[2] For people who (understanding the words) say that nothing matters are, it can safely be declared, giving but one example of that hypocrisy or *mauvaise foi* which Existentialists are fond of castigating.

I am not saying that no *philosophical* problem arises for the person who is perplexed by the peculiar logical character of the word "matters": there is one, and it is a real problem. There are no pseudo-problems in philosophy; if anything causes philosophical perplexity, it is the philosopher's task to find the cause of this perplexity and so remove it. My Swiss friend was not a hypocrite. His trouble was that, through philosophical naïveté, he took for a real moral problem what was not a moral problem at all, but a philosophical one—a problem to be solved, not by an agonizing struggle with his soul, but by an attempt to understand what he was saying.

I am not denying, either, that there may be people who can sincerely say that very little matters to them, or even almost nothing. We should say that they are psychologically abnormal. But for the majority of us to become like this is a contingency so remote as to excite neither fear nor attraction; we just are not made like that. We are creatures who feel concern for things—creatures who think one course of action better than another and act accordingly. And I easily convinced my Swiss friend that he was no exception.

So then, the first thing I want to say in this talk is that you cannot annihilate values—not values as a whole. As a matter of empirical fact, a man is a valuing creature, and is likely to remain so. What may happen is that one set of values may get discarded and another set substituted; for indeed our scales of values are always changing, sometimes gradually, sometimes catastrophically. The suggestion that *nothing* matters naturally arises at times of perplexity like the present, when the claims upon our concern are so many and conflicting that we might indeed wish to be delivered from all of them at once. But this we are unable to do. The suggestion may have one of two opposite effects, one good and one bad. On the one hand, it may make us scrutinise more closely values to which we have given habitual allegiance, and decide whether we really prize them as much as we have been pre-

2. *Treatise,* I 4 vii.

tending to ourselves that we do. On the other, it may make us stop thinking seriously about our values at all, in the belief that nothing is to be preferred to anything else. The effect of this is not as might be thought, to overthrow our values altogether (that, as I have said, is impossible); it merely introduces a shallow stagnation into our thought about values. We content ourselves with the appreciation of those things, like eating, which most people can appreciate without effort, and never learn to prize those things whose true value is apparent only to those who have fought hard to reach it. . . .

13

John Wisdom,
"The Meanings of the Questions of Life,"
from *Paradox and Discovery*

John Wisdom, a "linguistic philosopher," born in 1904, was a follower of Wittgenstein. He held Wittgenstein's chair in Cambridge and wrote an influential series of essays on Other Minds, *as well as the essays collected in* Philosophy and Psychoanalysis *and* Paradox and Discovery.

When one asks "What is the meaning of life?" one begins to wonder whether this large, hazy and bewildering question itself has any meaning. Some people indeed have said boldly that the question has no meaning. I believe this is a mistake. But it is a mistake which is not without excuse. And I hope that by examining the excuse we may begin to remedy the mistake, and so come to see that whether or not life has a meaning it is not senseless to enquire whether it has or not. First, then, what has led some people to think that the whole enquiry is senseless?

There is an old story which runs something like this: A child asked an old man "What holds up the world? What holds up all things?" The old man answered "A giant." The child asked "And what holds up the giant? You must tell me what holds up the giant." The old man answered "An elephant." The child said, "And who holds up the elephant?" The old man answered "A tortoise." The child said "You still have not told me what holds up all things. For what holds up the tortoise?" The old man answered "Run away and don't ask me so many questions."

From this story we can see how it may happen that a question which looks very like sensible meaningful questions may turn out to be a senseless, meaningless one. Again and again when we ask "What supports this?" it is possible to give a sensible answer. For instance what

John Wisdom, "The Meanings of the Question of Life", in J. Wisdom, *Paradox and Discovery*, Oxford, Blackwell, 1965.

supports the top-most card in a house of cards? The cards beneath it which are in their turn supported by the cards beneath them. What supports all the cards? The table. What supports the table? The floor and the earth. But the question "What supports all things, absolutely all things?" is different. It is absurd, it is senseless, like the question "What is bigger than the largest thing in the world?" And it is easy to see why the question "What supports all things?" is absurd. Whenever we ask, "What supports thing A or these things A, B, C," then we can answer this question only by mentioning some thing other than the thing A or things A, B, C about which we asked "What supports it or them." We must if we are to answer the question mention something D other than those things which form the subject of our question, and we must say that this thing is what supports them. If we mean by the phrase "all things" absolutely all things which exist then obviously there is nothing outside that about which we are now asked "What supports all this?" Consequently any answer to the question will be self-contradictory just as any answer to the question "What is bigger than the biggest of all things" must be self-contradictory. Such questions are absurd, or, if you like, silly and senseless.

In a like way again and again when we ask "What is the meaning of this?" we answer in terms of something other than this. For instance imagine that there has been a quarrel in the street. One man is hitting another man on the jaw. A policeman hurries up. "Now then" he says, "what is the meaning of all this?" He wants to know what led up to the quarrel, what caused it. It is no good saying to the policeman "It's a quarrel." He knows there is a quarrel. What he wants to know is what went before the quarrel, what led up to it. To answer him we must mention something other than the quarrel itself. Again suppose a man is driving a motor car and sees in front of him a road sign, perhaps a red flag, perhaps a skull and cross bones. "What does this mean?" he asks and when he asks this he wants to know what the sign points to. To answer we must mention something other than the sign itself, such as a dangerous corner in the road. Imagine a doctor sees an extraordinary rash on the face of his patient. He is astonished and murmurs to himself "What is the meaning of this?" He wants to know what caused the strange symptoms, or what they will lead to, or both. In any case in order to answer his question he must find something which went before or comes after and lies outside that about which he asks "What does this mean?" This need to look before or after in order to answer a question of the sort "What is the meaning of this?"

is so common, so characteristic, a feature of such questions that it is natural to think that when it is impossible to answer such a question in this way then the question has no sense. Now what happens when we ask "What is the meaning of life?"

Perhaps someone here replies, the meaning, the significance of this present life, this life on earth, lies in a life hereafter, a life in heaven. All right. But imagine that some persistent enquirer asks, "But what I am asking is what is the meaning of all life, life here and life beyond, life now and life hereafter? What is the meaning of all things in earth and heaven?" Are we to say that this question is absurd because there cannot be anything beyond all things while at the same time any answer to "What is the meaning of all things?" must point to some thing beyond all things?

Imagine that we come into a theatre after a play has started and are obliged to leave before it ends. We may then be puzzled by the part of the play that we are able to see. We may ask "What does it mean?" In this case we want to know what went before and what came after in order to understand the part we saw. But sometimes even when we have seen and heard a play from the beginning to the end we are still puzzled and still ask what does the whole thing mean. In this case we are not asking what came before or what came after, we are not asking about anything outside the play itself. We are, if you like, asking a very different sort of question from that we usually put with the words "What does this mean?" But we are still asking a real question, we are still asking a question which has sense and is not absurd. For our words express a wish to grasp the character, the significance of the whole play. They are a confession that we have not yet done this and they are a request for help in doing it. Is the play a tragedy, a comedy or a tale told by an idiot? The pattern of it is so complex, so bewildering, our grasp of it still so inadequate, that we don't know what to say, still less whether to call it good or bad. But this question is not senseless.

In the same way when we ask "What is the meaning of all things?" we are not asking a senseless question. In this case, of course, we have not witnessed the whole play, we have only an idea in outline of what went before and what will come after that small part of history which we witness. But with the words "What is the meaning of it all?" we are trying to find the order in the drama of Time. The question may be beyond us. A child may be able to understand, to grasp a simple play and be unable to understand and grasp a play more complex and more subtle. We do not say on this account that when he asks of the larger more complex play "What does it mean?" then his question is senseless, nor even that it is senseless for him. He has asked and even answered such a question in simpler cases, he knows the sort of effort, the sort of movement of the mind which such a question calls for, and we do not say that a question is meaningless to him merely because he is not yet able to carry out quite successfully the movement of that sort which is needed in order to answer a complex question of that sort. We do not say that a question in mathematics which is at present rather beyond us is meaningless to us. We know the type of procedure it calls for and may make efforts which bring us nearer and nearer to an answer. We are able to find the meaning which lies not outside but within very complex but still limited wholes whether these are dramas of art or of real life. When we ask "What is the meaning of all things?" we are bewildered and have not that grasp of the order of things the desire for which we express when we ask that question. But this does not render the question senseless nor make it impossible for us to move forwards an answer.

We must however remember that what one calls answering such a question is not giving an answer. I mean we cannot answer such a question in the form: "The meaning is this."

Such an idea about what form answering a question must take may lead to a new despair in which we feel we cannot do anything in the way of answering such a question as "What is the meaning in it all?" merely because we are not able to sum up our results in a phrase or formula.

When we ask what is the meaning of this play or this picture we cannot express the understanding which this question may lead to in the form of a list of just those things in the play or the picture which give it its meaning. No. The meaning eludes such a list. This does not mean that words quite fail us. They may yet help us provided that we do not expect of them more than they can do.

A person who is asked what he finds so hateful or so lovable in another may with words help himself and us in grasping what it is that so moves him. But he will only mislead us and himself if he pretends that his words are a complete account of all that there is in the matter.

It is the same when we ask what is it in all things that makes it all so good, so bad, so grand, so contemptible. We must not anticipate that the answer can be given in a word or in a neat list. But this does not mean that we can do nothing towards answering these questions nor even that words will not help us. Indeed surely the historians, the scientists, the prophets, the dramatists and the poets have said much which will help any man who asks himself: Is the drama of time meaningless as a tale told by an idiot? Or is it not meaningless? And if it is not meaningless is it a comedy or a tragedy, a triumph or a disaster, or is it a mixture in which sweet and bitter are for ever mixed?

14

A. J. Ayer,
"The Meaning of Life,"
from *The Meaning of Life*

A. J. Ayer, who died in 1989, was born in 1910. He was the best known and most iconoclastic philosopher of his generation. He brought logical positivism to England in his bombshell book Language, Truth and Logic, *published in 1936, when he was only twenty-six, arguing that metaphysical statements are meaningless because they are unverifiable.*

There are many ways in which a person's life may come to have a meaning for him in itself. He may find fulfilment in his work, though this cannot be guaranteed to last until old age. The same is true of the satisfaction which some people find in their domestic lives, with the factor of children and grandchildren playing its part. The English, of all classes, have not been noted in the past for the affection which they have commonly shown towards their children, or indeed received from them, but there have been exceptions and they may be on the increase. There are hobbies, like chess or stamp collecting, which may become a passion. I am not suggesting that these activities are of equal worth but only that they may be equally absorbing. Some people are absorbed in making money, presumably in most cases for the sake of the luxury, prestige, or power that the possession of it brings, but in some cases simply for its own sake; I know of a man who having set himself the goal of making a million pounds by the time he had attained a relatively youthful age could think of nothing better to do than set out to make another. His life might have been more interesting if he had been less sure of success. It lacked the spice which the fear of ruin gives to the life of the gambler. Again, I am not saying that the life of a gambler is morally preferable to that of a shrewd investor but only that it may be a life of greater intensity.

From *The Meaning of Life*, by A. J. Ayer, Weidenfeld & Nicolson. Reprinted with permission of the publisher.

One of the most conspicuous elements in what counts and has long counted in many societies for most people as a meaningful life is the pursuit and still more the acquisition of fame. This has increased its importance in the present century because the improvement of communication, the diffusion throughout the world of many of the same programmes on television and the cinema, has spread fame much more widely. It is also ephemeral. Pop stars drop out of fashion and questionnaires reveal a surprising ignorance of what one might have thought were household names. I wonder, for example, what percentage of Asians could name either the Prime Minister of England, or the President of the United States. I think it might turn out to be surprisingly small.

In general, people who desire fame also wish to be thought to deserve it. They wish that their work should be esteemed by those whom they regard as persons best qualified to judge it, preferably in their lifetime when they can be awarded honour and gratified by praise, but also after their death. Sometimes those who are neglected in their lifetime take consolation in the thought that its merits will eventually be recognized. 'On me lira vers 1880,' said Stendhal in the 1830s and how right he was. Of those who are recognized in their lifetime, I think many attach more importance to the hope that their work will endure and their names be honoured as the authors of it.

Yet there is something irrational about this. It is comprehensible that if one has created an outstanding work of art, of whatever kind, or hit upon an original scientific theory, or written good poetry, or a novel of unusual depth, or even made some contribution to philosophy, one should wish the outcome to continue to be appreciated. But why should it matter that one's name be attached to it? After all one is not going to know anything about it. One runs no risk of suffering the humiliation of Max Beerbohm's Enoch Soames or the triumph that he would have felt if he had found a eulogistic record of his name in the British Museum's catalogue. All the same it does matter. I have the hope that some of my work will continue to be read after my death, perhaps even here and there in a hundred year's time. Yet I do not care at all for the idea that it will be attributed to one of my colleagues, however much I may like or admire him. Perhaps I should prefer that someone else should get the credit for my work, than that it should vanish without trace, but I cannot honestly say that this is a matter of indifference to me. If the work survives, I want my name also to survive as its author. Yet it is not a pleasure that I shall enjoy. I shall have no means of telling whether it has survived or not.

Nevertheless, my friends and my children and my grandchildren, if I have any, will know that it has survived; and the belief that they will take pride in the fact is a source of satisfaction to me. I think that this is true, though its importance may be overestimated. A childless curmudgeon may equally relish the thought of his posthumous fame. Moreover, it is a motive which does not reach far into the future. I care a great deal for my son, my stepdaughter and her three-year-old child, but the idea that persons in the twenty-fourth century will take any pleasure in my being their ancestor carries no weight with me. It is a matter of indifference to me, and I expect to most other people, if they think about it honestly, whether or not their family line continues for another three hundred years.

So far, I have been speaking about the satisfaction that people receive for the character and conduct of their personal lives. But for the most part when questions are raised about the meaning of life, they do not look for an answer at this level. The problem which is posed is much more general. Does the existence of the universe serve any purpose, and if it does serve a purpose, does the existence of human beings enter into it? There is a tendency to assume that an affirmative answer to the first question entails an affirmative answer to the second, but this need not be so. If any sense can be made of the statement that the universe has a purpose, then the purpose could be one in which the existence of human beings played no part. Admittedly, those who cleave to the superstition of determinism, are committed to holding that the original organization of the world causally necessitates the emergence of human beings, but even they are not obliged to attach value to this outcome. They could regard us as an excrescence on the scheme of things.

Nevertheless the vast majority of those who believe that the universe serves a purpose do so because they take this as conferring a meaning on life. How far down in the scale of organisms are they prepared to go is not always clear. The hymnodist Mrs Alexander boldly strikes out with 'All things bright and beautiful, All creatures great and small, All things wise and wonderful, the Lord God made them all.' The first and third lines seem to allow for a good many omissions, but perhaps the second line makes up for them. Everything after all must have some size.

We must not overlook the last line of the stanza. Not all theories that the world has a destiny are theistic. There are conceptions of the governance of all things, and of men in particular, by an impersonal fate. Nevertheless, the notion of human life as owing its meaning to its playing its part in a grand design is most commonly associated with the belief that the universe was created by a being of supernatural intelligence, and it is this belief that I now intend to discuss.

Let me begin by saying that I totally reject it. In my youth, when I published my first book, I argued with some force that the concept of a transcendent deity was literally nonsensical. Now I am prepared to be a little more conciliatory. I am, indeed, in doubt, whether the notion of an incorporeal subject of consciousness is logically coherent, but as a follower of Hume I am prepared to envisage a series of experiences which are not linked in the ordinary way with experiences of a physical body. The problem which he and the rest of us have failed to solve is to fashion an adequate criterion of identity for such a series. But let that pass. The hypothesis then would be that the course of nature, including the emergence of human beings and the vicissitudes of their individual lives, was planned by the owner of this disembodied consciousness. There are indeed, difficulties about time, since a series of experiences presumably occurs in time and therefore must be antecedent to whatever our cosmologists light upon as the first physical event, if any. The series of psychical events, if deified, presumably had no beginning, which is not an easy conclusion to accept. But the difficulties of embracing either side of Kant's antinomy that the world had or that it had not a beginning in time are notorious, and they are not lessened by assuming time to start off with the world's alleged creator.

Fortunately, we need not become entangled in them. The hypothesis of there being a creator, even if it is allowed to be intelligible, fails through its being vacuous. To have any content it would need to specify the end for which the world was designed and the way in which various features of it promote this end. But this it does not even attempt to do. The so-called argument from design owed its popularity to the occurrence of teleological processes within the world; the adaptation of animal and human organs, such as those of sight and hearing, to their functions, the pollination of flowers, the dependence of parasites upon their hosts, phenomena now explained, more or less adequately, by the theory of natural selection. What was overlooked, except by some philosophers such as Hume in his *Dialogues Concerning Natural Religion*, was that the analogy of a watch and a watchmaker, or a building and its architect, apart from its internal imperfections, since neither watchmakers nor architects are incorporeal, simply does not apply to the universe as a whole. From what we know of it, the universe bears no resemblance to a clock or any other artefact. It has some structure, since anything that we are capable of describing must have some structure or other, but not any structure that the hypothesis of a creator prescribes. Whatever happens, the believer in the creator is going to say that that was what was intended. And just for this reason his hypothesis is vacuous.

'It can't all just be a fluke,' a young philosopher said to me the other day. On the contrary a fluke is all that it can be. I do not know how much that goes on is capable of explanation. I suspect rather less than we are apt to assume. But let us be optimistic. Let us suppose that we command a physiological theory which accounts for all the phenomena of consciousness in terms of processes in the central nervous system, and let us suppose that this theory is derivable from some biochemical theory, and so along the line until we come to relativity theory and the subatomic theories of contemporary physics. And let us suppose that we realize Einstein's vision of integrating them. What have we then? A set of formulae that are at best contingently true. They happen to account for the phenomena, as they are so far known to us, and maybe they will continue to do so. Or maybe they will need to be modified, as their predecessors have been. It makes no difference which way it goes. In either case the phenomena are what they are and the theories are adapted to them. Both could logically have been otherwise.

Suppose now, what we have seen to be false, that sense could be made of ascribing these theories to the intentions of a supernatural being. That too would make no serious difference. We should still end up with a fluke. For the fact that the world was ordered in the way it is rather than some other, if not due to the limitation of his capacity, must simply be put down to his whim.

Though they commonly go together, religious belief and belief in an afterlife, not taking the form of reincarnation, are logically distinct. I know of two atheists, both of them Cambridge philosophers, one of whom, J. Ellis McTaggart, was quite certain that he would survive, since he held the strange metaphysical view that everything in the world was a disguised immortal soul, and the other, C. D. Broad, whose interest in psychical research led him to believe that there was about an even chance of his surviving. What is curious about Broad is that he had no wish for this to happen. He thought poorly of this world and believed that the next world, if there was one, was quite likely to be even nastier.

I cannot claim to have gone deeply into the subject of psychical research, but such evidence as I have seen of what it has yielded has not seemed to be strong enough to overcome the main objections to the idea of one's surviving one's death; first the unsolved logical difficulty of defining personal identity in anything other than physical terms; and perhaps more importantly the abundant evidence which goes to show that all our conscious experiences are causally dependent upon our brains. I have already admitted that we do not have a set of well-established psychophysical hypotheses which correlate experiences one to one with states of the brain but the evidence for the overall, dependence of consciousness upon the brain is very strong.

Even if life had a meaning in the sense that we have just been discussing, it would not be known to the persons who had faith in it, nor would they have any inkling of the part that their own lives played in the overall plan. It might, therefore, seem surprising that the question was so important to them. Why should it matter to them that they followed a course which was not of their own choosing as a means to an end of which they were ignorant? Why should they derive any satisfaction from the belief that they were puppets in the hands of a superior agent?

I believe the answer is that most people are excited by the feeling that they are involved in a larger enterprise, even if they have no responsibility for its direction. This is a dangerous propensity since it makes them easier to manipulate, and so facilitates the growth of political and religious fanaticism. On the other hand, it can also serve the promotion of good causes, such as the agitation in favour of the victims of political injustice, or the organization of relief for the inhabitants of areas of famine. The case of war is an interesting example. I can speak, from experience, only of the second Great War, and only from an English point of view. I took part in it first as a soldier and then as a member of departments of intelligence. I suppose that I spent no more than half my time in England but it included the period of the blitz and that in which the V 1 rockets were replaced by the V 2s. The feature of this war, which concerns my argument, is that the civilian population was involved in it to a greater degree than in any previous war and certainly to a greater degree than they ever will be again, if our present strategy is maintained. As a result, it was apparent that they were living with a greater intensity, and also displaying in

manner and action a greater amount of fellow feeling than they pre-
viously had or would have again. It may sound shocking, but I honestly
believe that, with the exception of those who suffered personal injury
or personal loss, especially in the form of death or maiming of those
whom they loved, most English people enjoyed the war.

This is allied to the fact that if we take the intensity with which a
life is lived as a criterion of its being meaningful we shall find no very
close correlation between meaningful lives and those that we consider
morally estimable. The same will be true if we attribute meaning to
the lives of those who pass for having been great men or women,
especially if their greatness consisted in their power. I do not know
whether Lord Acton was justified in saying that great men are almost
always bad, but it is certainly not the case that they have always been
good. We need only think of Alexander the Great, Augustus Caesar,
Jenghis Kahn, Cesare Borgia, Martin Luther, Peter the Great, Cather-
ine the Great, Louis xiv, Florence Nightingale, John Pierpont Morgan,
Lord Beaverbrook and David Lloyd George. I have avoided bringing
the list up to date with Hitler and Stalin, in order to avoid the question
whether we are going so to construe greatness that causing an inordinate
amount of evil strips one of the title. There will still be no denying
that they were major historical figures and I suspect that, on the whole,
they were satisfied with their lives, Hitler at least until his last days
and even then he seems to have seen the collapse of his fortunes more
as the failure of the German people than his own; Stalin quite probably
until the very end, since even if he was poisoned he was not aware
of it.

In the realm of the arts, the disparity is not so flagrant, but still there
is no positive correlation between being a great artist and an amiable
man. Wagner is perhaps the most obvious counterexample. There is
little correlation between goodness and happiness. If virtue is said to
be its own reward it is because it so often acquires no other. As the
Psalmist put it, it is the ungodly whom one sees 'flourishing like a
green bay-tree'. In speaking of the ungodly I am not straying into
deism. I am not even thinking of major criminals, who quite often
come to grief, but of the multitude of minor villains who appear to
have come to the fore in recent years, persons skilled in sharp practice
on the stock exchange, hooligans, racists of one or other colour, persons
whose principal aim is not merely to keep up with the Jones's but to
outstrip them without being too scrupulous about the means.

The obvious disparity between virtue and prosperity in this world troubled the philosopher Immanuel Kant. He believed that there ought to be another world in which this balance would be redressed and thereby discovered a motive for believing in a God who would bring this about. I use the word 'motive' rather than 'reason' because, much as I dislike Kant's moral philosophy, I have too much respect for his intelligence to suppose that he regarded his pious hope as a serious argument. After all, it was Kant who first demolished the tricky ontological argument for the existence of God, the surprisingly durable pretence that the existence of a necessary being can be established by smuggling the factor of necessity into some grandiose concept, and went on to dispose with equal ease of the argument from design and the argument to a first cause.

My reasons for disliking Kant's moral philosophy are not only technical, inasmuch as he never succeeds in finding a way to bring his goodwill into action, but also moral. I do not care for the supremacy which he accords to the sense of duty over every human sympathy or principle of altruism. In his theory, indeed, it is only the sense of duty that counts. This is because he believed, mistakenly, that to act or fail to act in accordance with it lies in our power, in a way that the possession of the motives for other forms of action and our responses to them do not. In fact, actions done from a sense of duty are no less subject to causal conditioning than any others. Does the extent to which our actions are causally conditioned rob them of their moral value? I think not. I think that acts of cruelty or kindness are ugly or attractive in themselves, irrespective of their being correlated, in some measure, with states of our central nervous system, or explicable, however vaguely, in terms of our genetic endowment and the stimuli to which we have been subjected. This question is more difficult when it is directed towards the agent. Our ordinary moral judgments imply that he could not only have acted but in many cases chosen otherwise and it is not entirely clear to me what this means. I am inclined to think that the concept of desert which is included in our notion of moral responsibility is incoherent, but this is not a question into which I can enter here.

If I say that there are no such things as objective moral values, this is not to be taken as a profession of moral nihilism. I am not endorsing any moral principle that anybody happens to hold, still less alleging that all actions are morally neutral. On the contrary, I have strong moral sentiments and am anxious that other people should share them and act upon them. In saying that moral values are not objective, I am maintaining only that moral terms, while as it were, commenting on natural features of the world, do no themselves describe them. One consequence of this is that moral argument, in so far as it is not a dispute about some matter of fact, say, an agent's motive or the physical character of his action, is possible only on the basis of some common sentiment. For this reason, it is commonly *ad hominem*. One endeavours to convince one's opponent that his standpoint commits him to endorsing a course of action of which one is sure that he cannot honestly approve.

Evidently, there is no general answer to the question what constitutes a meaningful life. A life lived in one culture at a given social and economic level which satisfies one person might well fail to satisfy another who dwelt in a different or even in the same environment. Treating the question subjectively one can say, platitudinously, that it is a matter of the degree to which one achieves self-fulfilment. Treating it objectively, it is a matter of one's standing in one's society and the historical influence, if any, that one exerts. We have seen that the results of these different viewpoints need not coincide either with each other or with what we humane and liberal persons would regard as morally commendable.

I conclude with a question to which I do not know the answer. How far should our judgment of the worth of a person's life be affected by the fact that we take it to be based upon an illusion? Let us take the example of a nun, belonging to a strict order, leading a life of austerity, but serene in the performance of her devotions, confident that she is loved by her deity, and that she is destined for a blissful future in the world to come. If this example is considered to be too subjective, we can allot her a position of authority in the convent and locate her at a time and place when abbesses were historically important. It makes no difference to the problem. The question is whether it matters that the deity in whose love she rejoices does not exist and that there is no world to come.

I am inclined to say that it does matter, just as G. E. Moore in the last chapter of *Principia Ethica* goes so far as to say that 'a merely poetical contemplation of the Kingdom of Heaven *would* be superior to that of the religious believer, if it were the case (as he in fact thought it was) that the Kingdom of Heaven does not and will not really exist.'[1] I suppose that he was and I am yielding to what he called 'a strong

1. 2nd edn., p. 495.

respect for truth'. But what is our argument? It is not as if there were some end that the nun's life is failing to achieve. So far as one can survey the Universe *sub specie aeternitatis* one has to agree with Macbeth. It *is* 'a tale, told by an idiot, full of sound and fury, signifying nothing'. What is wrong with this quotation is its aura of disillusionment. It is not that we are sentenced to deprivation. It is open to us to make our lives as satisfying as our circumstances allow. But to return to the nun. It would indeed be terrible for her to discover that the point of her life was nonexistent. But *ex hypothesi* this is something that she will never know.

15

Moritz Schlick,
"On the Meaning of Life,"
from *Philosophical Papers*

Moritz Schlick (1882–1936) was the leader of the Vienna Circle, a group of philosophers which developed the doctrines of logical positivism. Among his works are the General Theory of Knowledge *and* Questions of Ethics. *He was assassinated by a student in 1936.*

Not everyone is disturbed by the question, whether life has a meaning. Some—and they are not the unhappiest—have the child's mind, which has *not yet* asked about such things; others *no longer* ask, having unlearnt the question. In between are ourselves, the seekers. We cannot project ourselves back to the level of the innocent, whom life has not yet looked at with its dark mysterious eyes, and we do not care to join the weary and the blasé, who no longer believe in any meaning to existence, because they have been able to find none in their own.

A man who has failed of the goal that his youth was striving for, and found no substitute, may lament the meaninglessness of his own life; yet he still may believe in a meaning to existence generally, and think that it continues to be found where a person has reached his goals. But the man who has wrested from fate the achievement of his purposes, and then finds that his prize was not so valuable as it seemed, that he has somehow fallen prey to a deception—that man is quite blankly confronted with the question of life's value, and before him lies like a darkened wasteland the thought, not only that all things pass, but also that everything is ultimately in vain.

How are we to discover a unitary meaning, either in the perplexities of a man's lifetime, or in the stumbling progress of history itself?

Moritz Schlick, "On the Meaning of Life", *Philosophical Papers* Vol. II (1925–1936), ed. Henk L. Mulder and Barbara F.B. van de Velde-Schlick, trans. P.L. Heath, Reidel, Holland, 1979.

Existence may appear to us as a many-hued tapestry, or as a grey veil, but it is equally difficult either way to furl the billowing fabric so that its meaning becomes apparent. It all flaps past and seems to have vanished before we could render an account of it.

What is the reason for the strange contradiction, that achievement and enjoyment will not fuse into a proper meaning? Does not an inexorable law of nature appear to prevail here? Man sets himself goals, and while he is heading towards them he is buoyed up by hope, indeed, but gnawed at the same time by the pain of unsatisfied desire. Once the goal is reached, however, after the first flush of triumph has passed away, there follows inevitably a mood of desolation. A void remains, which can seemingly find an end only through the painful emergence of new longings, the setting of new goals. So the game begins anew, and existence seems doomed to be a restless swinging to and fro between pain and boredom, which ends at last in the nothingness of death. That is the celebrated line of thought which Schopenhauer made the basis of his pessimistic view of life. Is it not possible, somehow, to escape it?

We know how Nietzsche, for example, sought to conquer this pessimism. First by the flight into art: consider the world, he says, as an aesthetic phenomenon, and it is eternally vindicated! Then by the flight into knowledge: look upon life as an experiment of the knower, and the world will be to you the finest of laboratories! But Nietzsche again turned away from these standpoints; in the end, art was no longer his watchword, and nor were science, or beauty, or truth; it is hard to reduce to a brief formula what the wisest Nietzsche, the Nietzsche of *Zarathustra*, saw as the meaning of life. For if it be said that henceforth the ultimate value of life, to him, was *life itself*, that obviously says nothing clear and does not find the right expression for the deep truth which he then perceived or at least suspected. For he saw that life has no meaning, so long as it stands wholly under the domination of purposes:

> Verily, it is a blessing and no blasphemy when I teach: Above all things standeth the heaven of chance, the heaven of innocence, the heaven of hazard, the heaven of sportiveness.
> 'Sir Hazard'—his is the most ancient title of nobility in earth: him have I restored to all things, I have saved them from the slavery of ends.
> This freedom and heavenly brightness I set over all things as an azure

dome, when I taught that above them and in them there willeth no 'eternal will'.[1]

In truth, we shall never find an ultimate meaning in existence, if we view it only under the aspect of purpose. I know not, however, whether the burden of purposes has ever weighed more heavily upon mankind than at the present time. The present idolizes work. But work means goal-seeking activity, direction to a purpose. Plunge into the crowd on a bustling city street and imagine yourself stopping the passers-by, one after another, and crying to them 'Where are you off to so fast? What important business do you have?' And if, on learning the immediate goal, you were to ask further about the purpose of this goal, and again for the purpose of that purpose, you would almost always hit on the purpose after just a few steps in the sequence: maintenance of life, earning one's bread. And why maintain life? To this question you could seldom read off an intelligible answer from the information obtained.

And yet an answer has to be found. For mere living, pure existence as such, is certainly valueless; it must also have a content, and in that only can the meaning of life reside. But what actually fills up our days almost entirely is activities serving to maintain life. In other words, the content of existence consists in the work that is needed in order to exist. We are therefore moving in a circle, and in this fashion fail to arrive at a meaning for life. Nor is it any better if, in place of work itself, we direct our attention to the fruits of work. The greater part of its products is again subservient to work of some kind, and hence indirectly to the maintenance of life, and another large part is undoubtedly meaningless trash. Rathenau, if I am not mistaken, estimated this latter at one third of total production. How much would be left as meaningful? Nor, indeed, can any work-products as such ever be valuable, save insofar as they somehow fulfil and enrich life, by launching man into valuable states and activities. The state of working cannot be one of these, for by work—if we understand this concept in its philosophical generality—we simply mean any activity undertaken solely in order to realize some purpose. It is therefore the characteristic

1. [*Also sprach Zarathustra*, Part 3. 'Vor Sonnenaufgang'; Engl. by A. Tille, revised by M. M. Bozman, 'Before Sunrise', in *Thus Spake Zarathustra*, London 1933, p. 148.]

mark of work that it has its purpose outside itself, and is not performed
for its own sake. The doctrine that would wish to install work as such
at the centre of existence, and exalt it to life's highest meaning, is
bound to be in error, because every work-activity as such is always a
mere means, and receives its value only from its goals.

The core and ultimate value of life can lie only in such states as
exist for their own sake and carry their satisfaction in themselves.
Now such states are undoubtedly given in the pleasure-feelings which
terminate the fulfilment of a volition and accompany the gratifying of
a desire; but if we sought to derive the value of existence from these
moments, in which life's pressure is momentarily halted, we should at
once become ensnared in that argument of Schopenhauer's, which
displays to us, not the meaning, but the absurdity of life.

No, life means movement and action, and if we wish to find a
meaning in it we must seek for *activities* which carry their own purpose
and value within them, independently of any extraneous goals; activities,
therefore, which are not work in the philosophical sense of the word.
If such activities exist, then in them the seemingly divided is reconciled,
means and end, action and consequence are fused into one, we have
then found ends-in-themselves which are more than mere end-points
of acting and resting-points of existence, and it is these alone that can
take over the role of a true content to life.

There really are such activities. To be consistent, we must call them
play, since that is the name for free, purposeless action, that is, action
which in fact carries its purpose within itself. We must take the word
'play', however, in its broad, true, philosophical meaning—in a deeper
sense than is commonly accorded to it in daily life. We are not thereby
lending it any new or surprising meaning, but are merely repeating
what was perfectly clear to at least one great mind, who apprehended
the nature of the human with the eye of a poet—which is to say, in
deep truth. For in his *Letters on the Aesthetic Education of Man*, Friedrich
Schiller utters the following words:

> For, to declare it once and for all, Man plays only when he is in the full
> sense of the word a man, and *he is only wholly Man when he is playing*. This
> proposition, which at the moment perhaps seems paradoxical, will assume
> great and deep significance when we have once reached the point of applying
> it to the twofold seriousness of duty and of destiny; it will, I promise you,
> support the whole fabric of aesthetic art, and the still more difficult art of
> living. But it is only in science that this statement is unexpected; it has long

since been alive and operative in Art, and in the feeling of the Greeks, its most distinguished exponents; only they transferred to Olympus what should have been realized on earth. Guided by its truth, they caused not only the seriousness and the toil which furrow the cheeks of mortals, but also the futile pleasure that smooths the empty face, to vanish from the brows of the blessed gods, and they released these perpetually happy beings from the fetters of every aim, every duty, every care, and made idleness and indifference the enviable portion of divinity; merely a more human name for the freest and sublimest state of being.[2]

These are exalted words, which ring down from the poet's world into a care-dimmed age, and in our own world sound untimely to most ears. The poet sees a state of divine perfection among men, in which all their activities are turned into joyous play, all their working-days become holidays. Only insofar as man shares in this perfection, only in the hours when life smiles at him without the stern frown of purpose, is he really man. And it was sober consideration that led us to this very truth: the meaning of existence is revealed only in play.

But doesn't this notion lead us into mere dreams, does it not loosen every tie with reality, and have we not lost beneath our feet the solid earth of daily life, on which we have ultimately to stay planted, since the question of life is by nature an everyday question? In the harsh reality, especially of the present, there seems no room for such dreams; for our age, for the peoples of a war-racked globe, no other solution seems possible save the word 'work', and it appears irresponsible to speak ill of it.

Yet we should not forget that the creation which the hour demands of us is work only in the economic sense, productive activity, that is, which leads to the engendering of values. There is, however, no irreconcilable opposition between play in the philosophical sense and work in the economic meaning of the term. Play, as we see it, is any activity which takes place entirely for its own sake, independently of its effects and consequences. There is nothing to stop these effects from being of a useful or valuable kind. If they are, so much the better; the action still remains play, since it already bears its own value within itself. Valuable goods may proceed from it, just as well as from intrinsi-

2. [*Über die ästhetische Erziehung des Menschen, in einer Reihe von Briefen*, 1795, no. 15; Engl. by R. Snell, *Letters on the Aesthetic Education of Man*, London 1954, p. 80.]

cally unpleasurable activity that strives to fulfil a purpose. Play too, in other words, can be creative; its outcome can coincide with that of work.

This notion of creative play will be accorded a major part in the life-philosophy of the future. If mankind is to go on existing and progressing by way of playful activities, they will have to be creative; the necessary must somehow be brought forth by means of them. And this is possible, since play is not a form of doing nothing. The more activities, indeed, become play in the philosophical sense, the more work would be accomplished in the economic sense, and the more values would be created in human society. Human action is work, not because it bears fruit, but only when it proceeds from, and is governed by, the thought of its fruit.

Let us look about us: where do we find creative play? The brightest example (which at the same time is more than a mere example), is to be seen in the creation of the artist. His activity, the shaping of his work by inspiration, is itself pleasure, and it is half by accident that enduring values arise from it. The artist may have no thought, as he works, of the benefit of these values, or even of his reward, since otherwise the act of creation is disrupted. Not the golden chain, but the song that pours from the heart, is the guerdon that richly rewards! So feels the poet, and so the artist. And anyone who feels thus in what he does, *is* an artist.

Take, for example, the scientist. *Knowing*, too, is a pure play of the spirit, the wrestling for scientific truth is an end-in-itself for him, he rejoices to measure his powers against the riddles which reality propounds to him, quite regardless of the benefits that may somehow accrue from this (and these, as we know, have often been the most astonishing precisely in the case of purely theoretical discoveries, whose practical utility no one could originally have guessed). The richest blessings flow from the work that is engendered as the child of its creator's happy mood, and in free play, without any anxious concern for its effects.

Not all the activity of the artist or thinker falls, of course, under the concept of creative play. The purely technical, the mere management of the material, as with the painter's colour-mixing, or the composer's setting-down of notes—all this remains, for the most part, toil and work; they are the husks and dross that often still attach to play in real life. Often, but not always; for in the process of execution the working acts involved can either become so mechanized that they hardly enter consciousness, or else develop so much charm and attractiveness that they turn into artistic play themselves.

And that is also true in the end of those actions which engender neither science nor art, but the day's necessities, and which are seemingly altogether devoid of spirit. The tilling of the fields, the weaving of fabrics, the cobbling of shoes, can all become play, and may take on the character of artistic acts. Nor is it even so uncommon for a man to take so much pleasure in such activities, that he forgets the purpose of them. Every true craftsman can experience in his own case this transformation of the means into an end-in-itself, which can take place with almost any activity, and which makes the product into a work of art. It is the joy in sheer creation, the dedication to the activity, the absorption in the movement, which transforms work into play. As we know, there is a great enchantment which almost always brings this transformation about—rhythm. To be sure, it will only work perfectly where it is not brought externally and deliberately to the activity, and artificially coupled with it, but evolves spontaneously from the nature of the action and its natural form. There are some kinds of work where this is impossible; many are of such a nature that they always remain an evil and—except, perhaps, among men entirely blunted and incapable of happiness—are invariably carried out with reluctance and distaste. With such occupations I advise a very careful scrutiny of their fruits: we shall invariably find that such mechanical, brutalizing, degrading forms of work serve ultimately to produce only trash and empty luxury. So away with them! So long, indeed, as our economy is focussed on mere increase of production, instead of on the true enrichment of life, these activities cannot diminish, and thus slavery among mankind (for these alone are true forms of slave-labour) will not be able to decline. But a civilization which maintains artificial breeding-grounds for idle trumpery by means of forced slave-labour, must eventually come to grief through its own absurdity. All that will then remain over will be simply the avocations serving to generate true culture. But in them there dwells a spirit that favours their evolution into true forms of play.

At least there is no law of nature which in any way obstructs such a development of action into an end-in-itself; basically speaking, the road lies open to the realization of Schiller's dream. The idea of a human race thus liberated from all tormenting purposes, all oppressive cares, and cheerfully dedicated to the moment, is at least not a contradictory or inconceivable idea. The individual would lead an existence, as in the profound and beautiful saying of the Bible, like the life of the lilies of the field.

The objection may be raised at this point, that such a life would represent a relapse to a lower level, to the status of plants and animals. For the latter assuredly live for the moment, their consciousness is confined to a brief present, they certainly know pain, but not care. Man, on the contrary, has the privilege of embracing long periods, whole lifetimes, in the span of his consciousness, of coexperiencing them through foresight and hindsight, and that is how he becomes the knowing, supremely self-conscious being, in which capacity he confronts all the rest of nature.

But this objection is easy to meet. Man does not have to forfeit the range of his life, his joy in the moment will not be blind and bestial, but bathed in the clearest light of consciousness. He does not escape the menace of purposes by putting his head in the sand, so as not to see the future at all; it stands behind him in the light of recollection. He can shake off the curse of purposes and liberate his vision from the blight of cares, without lessening the boon of his hopes. He still sees even the remotest consequences of his action clearly before him, and not only the real consequences, but all possible ones as well; but no specific goal stands there as an end to be necessarily attained, so that the whole road would be meaningless if it were not; every point, rather, of the whole road already has its own intrinsic meaning, like a mountain path that offers sublime views at every step and new enchantments at every turn, whether it may lead to a summit or not. The setting of certain goals is admittedly needed in order to produce the tension required for life; even playful activity is constantly setting itself tasks, most palpably in sport and competition, which still remains play so long as it does not degenerate into real fighting. But such goals are harmless, they impose no burden on life and do not dominate it; they are left aside and it does not matter if they are not achieved, since at any moment they can be replaced by others. Stretches of life that stand under the dominion of huge inexorable purposes are like riddles with an answer that we either find or fail at; but a life of play might be compared to an endless crossword puzzle, in which new words are constantly being found and connected, so that an ever larger area is progressively filled in, with no other aim but that of going on further without a halt.

The last liberation of man would be reached if in all his doings he could give himself up entirely to the act itself, inspired to his activity always by love. The end, then, would never justify the means, he might then exalt into his highest rule of action the principle: 'What is not worth doing for its own sake, don't do for anything else's sake!' All life would then be truly meaningful, down to its ultimate ramifications; to live would mean: to celebrate the festival of existence.

Plato, in the *Laws* (803c), had already declared that men should make play, song and dance, as the true divine worship, into the proper content of life. But though well over two thousand years have passed in the meantime, perhaps men were closer in those days to such an order of life than they are today. In the present age, assuredly, the daily activity of man can in large part be justified only by distant purposes. In itself such activity is unpleasurable and unjustified, and the deification of work as such, the great gospel of our industrial age, has been exposed as idolatry. The greater part of our existence, filled as it is with goal-seeking work at the behest of others, has no value in itself, but obtains this only by reference to the festive hours of play, for which work provides merely the means and the preconditions.

Unremitting stern fulfilment of duty in the service of an end eventually makes us narrow and takes away the freedom that everyone requires for self-development. We have to be able to breathe freely. Hence arises the task of releasing, for a day, an hour, a minute, at least, the life that is fettered in its entirety to the purposes of utility; and these hours and minutes, however few they may be, form the content for whose sake all the rest is there, and for whose sake all the rest is on occasion sacrificed. At bottom we find man always ready to give up the senseless remainder of life, for an hour that is filled with value.

Man's teachers and benefactors, his seers and leaders, can strive for nothing else but to permeate the broadest possible stretches of existence with meaning. The achievement of a John Ruskin was based on the idea that human life must allow of being shaped into a chain of festive acts; the daily round can be made meaningful if it is filled in every detail with beauty. If it is not possible to lead the whole of life on the bright side, we must at least be able to break surface from time to time. If it is not possible to realize Schiller's dream, there is all the more need to follow Goethe's rule of life: "Work by day, at evening guests, toilsome weeks and joyous feasts." In our own civilization, joyous feasts are not possible without toilsome weeks, but in no age is a lasting life possible without joy and festivities. A life that is constantly focussed only on distant goals eventually loses all power of creation whatsoever. It is like a bow that is always bent: in the end it can no longer loose off the arrow, and with that its tension becomes pointless. Work and toil, so long as they have not themselves become joyous play, should make joy and play possible; therein their meaning lies. But they cannot do it if man has forgotten how to rejoice, if festive hours do not see to it that the knowledge of what joy is, is retained.

Yet let us beware of confusing joy, on which life's value depends, with its surrogate, mere pleasure, that shallow enjoyment of which Schiller said that it smooths the empty face of mortals. Pleasure wearies, while joy refreshes; the latter enriches, the former puts a false sheen upon existence. Both, indeed, lead us away from daily toil and distract us from care, but they do it in different ways: pleasure by diverting us, joy by pulling us together. Diversion offers the spirit fleeting excitement, without depth or content; for joy there is more needed, a thought or feeling which fills the whole man, an inspiration which sets him soaring above everyday life. He can only joy whole-heartedly about things which completely take hold of him, he has to be utterly devoted to something. Pain is commended for deepening us (perhaps because otherwise we have nothing good to say of it), but true joy has a very much greater effect. Joy is deeper than heartache, says Nietzsche. Pleasure, however, merely ruffles the surface of the soul and leaves it as featureless as before; it even tends to silt up the soul, for it leaves behind a stale after-taste, as symptom of a spiritual turbidity. And by this, indeed, it can be distinguished from exalted joy, which is an affirmation of existence conferring meaning upon life.

Here we can learn from the *child*. Before he has yet been caught in the net of purposes, the cares of work are unknown to him; he needs no diversion or release from the working day. And it is precisely the child that is capable of the purest joy. People everywhere are wont to sing of the happiness of youth, and this is truly more than a mere invention of the poets; youth is really not overshadowed by the dark clouds of purpose.

And with that I come to the heart of what I should here like to say.

It is not in every expression of life, not in the whole breadth of it, that we are able to find a meaning—at least so long as Schiller's dream of divine perfection remains a mere dream; the meaning of the whole is concentrated and collected, rather, into a few short hours of deep, serene joy, into the hours of play. And these hours crowd thickest in *youth*. It is not only that childish games are play even in the philosophical sense of the term; it is also that later youth, which is already well acquainted with aims and purposes, and has been brought up to serve them, still does not stand entirely under their yoke, does not have its gaze fixed on them alone, is not concerned solely with attaining them, as is often the natural attitude later on. Youth, on the contrary, does not really care about purposes; if one collapses, another is quickly built up; goals are merely an invitation to rush in and fight, and this enterprising ardour is the true fulfilment of the youthful spirit. The enthusiasm of youth (it is basically what the Greeks called Eros), is devotion to the deed, not the goal. This act, this way of acting, is true play.

If it is clear in this fashion that what makes up the meaning of existence is nowhere so purely or strongly to be found as it is in youth, some notable questions and clues emerge from this. Youth, after all, is the first phase of life, and it seems incongruous that the meaning of the whole should be found only at its beginning. For according to the traditional view, life is to be regarded as a process of development, whose meaning is constantly unfolding, so that it ought to be most clearly apparent towards the end. What, then, is youth? On the received view it is the time of immaturity, in which mind and body grow, in order later to *have* grown up to their vocation; the time of learning, in which all capacities are exercised, in order to be equipped for work; even the play of youth appears from this angle as merely a preparation for the seriousness of life. It is almost always so regarded, and almost the whole of education is conducted from this point of view: it signifies a training for adulthood. Youth therefore appears as a mere means to the later purposes of life, as a necessary learning period, that would have no meaning of its own.

This view is directly opposed to the insight that we have obtained. It has seldom been remarked, what a paradox it is that the time of preparation appears as the sweetest portion of existence, while the time of fulfilment seems the most toilsome. At times, however, it has been seen. It was primarily Rousseau, and perhaps Montaigne before him, who discovered the intrinsic value of youth. He warns the educator against debasing the youth of the pupil into a mere means and sacrificing his early happiness to later proficiency; the aim should be to fill the days of youth with joy, even for their own sake. At the present day this idea has begun to make a little headway. It is a leading conception of the modern youth movement, that a young life is not only going to receive its value from the future, but bears it within itself. Youth, in fact, is not just a time of growing, learning, ripening and incompleteness, but primarily a time of play, of doing for its own sake, and hence a true bearer of the meaning of life. Anyone denying this, and regarding youth as a mere introduction and prelude to real life, commits the same error that beclouded the mediaeval view of human existence: he shifts life's centre of gravity forwards, into the future. Just as the majority of religions, discontented with earthly life, are wont to transfer the meaning of existence out of this life and into a hereafter, so man in general is inclined always to regard every state, since none of them is wholly perfect, as a mere preparation for a more perfect one.

For modern man there is little doubt that the value and aim of life must either be totally of this world, or else cannot be found at all. And if man were to run through a thousand successive lives, as the theories of transmigration maintain, this world not absolve contemporary thought from seeking in every one of these stages of existence its own special meaning, independent of what has gone before or is yet to follow. Present-day man would have no right to look upon other, metaphysical worlds, if they existed, as superior or more meaningful, and ungratefully to despise our own world by comparison. The meaning of the life that he knows can only be sought in this world *as* he knows it.

But within life he now commits the same mistake that he committed earlier in thinking of its metaphysical continuation: from immature youth he shifts the value of life into mature adulthood; in his prime, he sees that he is still not yet ripe, that his nature and achievements are not complete, and therefore shifts the meaning of life still further on, and expects it from the peace and mellowness of old age. But on actually arriving at this peace, he then projects the meaning of existence backwards again into the days of acting and striving, and these are by then over and past recovery. And the final result is that man lets his whole life fall under the curse of purposes. It is the unceasing search into the future and concern for the future that casts its shadow over every present and clouds the joy of it.

But if life has a meaning, it must lie in the present, for only the present is real. There is no reason at all, however, why more meaning should lie in the later present, in the middle or final period of life, than in an earlier present, in the first period, known as youth. And now let us consider what 'youth' must actually mean for us in this connection. We found its true nature, not in the fact that it is a prelude and first phase of life, but rather in that it is the time of play, the time of activity for the pleasure of acting. And we recognized that all action, even the creative action of the adult, can and must, in its perfect form, take on the same character: it becomes play, self-sufficient action that acquires its value independently of the purpose.

But from this it follows that youth, in our philosophical sense, can by no means be confined to the early stages of life; it is present wherever the state of man has reached a peak, where his action has become play, where he is wholly given over to the moment and the matter in hand. We talk in such cases of youthful enthusiasm, and that is the right expression: enthusiasm is always youthful. The ardour which fires us for a cause, a deed or a man, and the ardour of youth, are one and the same fire. A man who is emotionally immersed in what he does is a youngster, a child. The great confirmation of this is genius, which is always imbued with a child-like quality. All true greatness is full of a deep innocence. The creativity of genius is the play of a child, his joy in the world is the child's pleasure in pretty things. Heraclitus of old it was who compared the creative world-spirit itself to a child at play, building things out of pebbles and bits of wood and tearing them down again. For us, therefore, the word 'youth' does not have the external meaning of a specific period of life, a particular span of years; it is a state, a way of leading one's life, which basically has nothing to do with years and the number of them.

It will now no longer be possible to misunderstand me when, as the heart of what I am moved to say, I assert the proposition that *the meaning of life is youth.*

The more youth is realized in a life, the more valuable it is, and if a person dies young, however long he may have lived, his life has had meaning. In the concept of youth, so viewed, there is an infinite abundance; an infinite abundance can be extracted from it. All values of existence can be set in relation to it. In my leisure hours I have been occupied with working out a 'Philosophy of Youth',[3] which is meant to show how every perfection whatever, in all areas of human existence, and perhaps not there alone, can be covered by the concept of youthfulness.

It was earlier the custom to group human values around three great

3. [Of the *Philosophy of Youth* only a fragment of the first chapter (about 25 typewritten pages) was found among Schlick's papers. Its title is 'Spiel, die Seele der Jugend' ('Play, the Soul of Youth'). The cover lists the titles of two projected further chapters: 'Schönheit, das Antlitz der Jugend' ('Beauty, the Countenance of Youth') and 'Adel, das Herz der Jugend' ('Nobility, the Heart of Youth').]

centres: the beautiful, the good and the true. The three faculties of feeling, willing and thinking, and the three cultural areas of art, society and enquiry, were held to correspond to them. In all these triads the connection with the value of youth can easily be pointed out, by showing how at their highest level the exercise of these different faculties becomes play. As a fact, we find art and the beautiful in the pure devotion to feeling for its own sake; immersion in thinking for its own sake gives rise to knowledge and science; and so far as the good is concerned, it can be reduced to a certain harmony of human impulses, whereby willing, too, becomes a joyous game, without disagreeable struggles and hindrances due to the threatening injunctions and prohibitions imposed by purpose.

The beautiful and the theory of beauty are already by nature wide open to examination from the viewpoint attained. For we only have to utter the word 'youth' and the idea of 'beauty' arises quite spontaneously. And if we look for the link that couples the two together, we eventually light on the concept of the playful, as the harmonious and self-sufficient, to which every external purpose is foreign; and the old question of the relations of the purposive to the beautiful could thence find a simple solution. An object cannot appear beautiful without being detached from purposive connection with the necessities of life. The conditions under which such detachment occurs in reality are laws of *natural* beauty; but *art* possesses means of liberating *any* object in this fashion, and hence there is nothing that it could not make beautiful by its depiction. It has long since become clear to us that artistic *creation* must be understood by way of the concept of play; but this is naturally true of the *enjoyment* of art as well, and above all of the meaning of the beautiful for human existence. Beauty is so much a part of the meaning of life, that without it the latter would simply be turned into absurdity. And the beautiful, the harmony of lines and colours and sounds and feelings, is the purest manifestation of play, of the mark of youth. The more youthful the art and the work of art, the greater their perfection; the more antiquated and pedantic, the more disagreeable and senseless they become.

But the highest beauty can never reside in the work of art, so long as it stands contrasted, as an artifact, to nature and life. The enjoyment of artistic beauty is play at second hand, through the medium of the work as an artificial plaything. But beauty can enter into life itself, without requiring a medium. When the beautiful form of the work of art migrates into life, we have reached the higher level of beauty, and the art of works of art, which represents a turning-away from, or (as Nietzsche calls it) a mere appendage of life, becomes superfluous. It has justly been said (by Wyneken), that "in a perfect world, there would be no art". And indeed, when rightly regarded, our art is but nostalgia for nature, for a better nature, and could be extinguished by a life filled with beauty. No one has proclaimed this truth more ardently than the brilliant and fertile philosopher Guyau, who died in 1888 at the age of thirty-three. For him it is merely an unwelcome and quite untypical restriction of art, to be a recreation from the struggle for existence, and a simulacrum of what moves us in real life. On the contrary, it is just the eternal affliction of the artist, that he cannot become one with the whole fullness of life, that he does not experience everything he depicts, but must sink himself in looking and portraying. The goal would be to take up beauty wholly into active life; the latter would then be stripped of that remainder of purposive work, without which, in our actual existence, no work of art comes into being . . . beauty would then have secured its full share in the meaning of life, our existence would glow with the indescribable freshness of youth.

That youthfulness of life enriches it in meaning by filling it with beauty, will be readily conceded; but if I maintain that it also fills life with *goodness*, that the ethos and moral quality of life is no less intimately connected with youth and play, it will be harder to find credence. And yet this is the most important point of all. For the ethical is after all the true heart of life, and here its deepest meaning must be sought. It is, however, the general opinion, that youth, properly speaking, is beyond good and evil, that morality begins only with responsibility, and responsibility only with that seriousness which is alien to youth and the very opposite of play. The concept of *duty*, which so many philosophers place at the centre of their ethics, presupposes the concept of purpose; to obey the commands of duty means nothing else but to stand under the dominion of purposes. Could there be no truth in what such wise and excellent men have taught: that the meaning of life must be found in the performance of our duty? It is not easy to reconcile what seems such a violent conflict of views, and to discern what is wisdom, and what prejudice, in this moral doctrine of duty.

Let us recall Schiller's remark, that the principle of play as the tue vocation of man will attain its deepest significance if we apply it to the seriousness of duty and destiny. What does this mean? It was Schiller who rebelled against the doctrine of Kant, whereby, of course, the moral is primarily to be found where man acts by conquering himself.

For in Kant's view an action is moral only when it springs from reverence for the law of duty as its sole motive; and since in the actual man conflicting inclinations are always present, moral action means a struggle against one's own inclination, it means laborious work. Schiller was utterly and entirely right, for this account of the good is infinitely remote from the meaning that everyone is otherwise naturally accustomed to associate with the word. We do not call *him* the best man, who is obliged unceasingly to resist his own impulses and is constantly at war with his own desires; we say this, rather, of the man whose inclinations are kindly and benevolent from the start, so that he simply does not fall into doubt and self-conflict. The man who struggles with and conquers himself is perhaps the type of the *great* man, but not of the *good* one. A being whose pure will flows from his natural disposition, without reflection or hesitation or wavering, is what we call an innocent person, and innocence is always the state of greatest moral perfection. This innocence is thus by no means a kind of ignorance, but rather a kind of freedom. It belongs inseparably to youth. There is the deepest wisdom in the biblical injunction: "Unless ye become as little children ... ". Where no exertion is required, where, without fear or wavering a man does freshly from the heart what is suited to his nature, there he is simply young, however many years he may number; his will, in such a case, is a free play in which he rejoices for its own sake, without looking onward to distant goals or upward to exalted duties. He acts out of pleasure in the good deed, he is good in himself, so far as he is youthful. But so far as it costs him trouble and exertion, his soul is an elderly one.

How long will it yet take until we eradicate the great moral prejudice, that seriousness and duty are a necessary part of the concept of morality, and until the ethics of duty is superseded by a natural ethics of goodness? In current morality the ethical is distorted and sicklied o'er with age, hedged about with scruples, constrained on all sides with anxious prohibitions, robbed of its naturalness and reduced to a serious matter, which every philistine can prate about. But true virtue is joyful, it does not arise from the pressure of prohibitions and purposes, but evolves freely from willing. Child-like purity is more beautiful and perfect than heroic renunciation. Jean Paul said: "As the eagle soars high above the highest mountains, so a right love surpasses the rugged path of duty." But love and youth are as much akin as youth and beauty.

Thus ethical perfection can be traced back to youthfulness. Just as, in Emerson's words, age is the only real sickness, so it is also the source of all moral evil, if, from the philosophical viewpoint, we do but regard age as nothing else but subjection to the burden of purposes. From rumination about the purposes of action the badness in the moral world arises; the entry of goal-seeking into life, and involvement in the network of purposes, betokens the loss of innocence, the true fall of man. It is a deeply tragic drama to see how the freshness of youthful life is increasingly palsied by the incursion of purposes, how its relation to the human environment increasingly forfeits the character of play, and guilt becomes possible. The childish self, which at first is not clearly aware of its limits vis-à-vis the environment, gradually becomes surrounded by a boundary, beyond which the world confronts him as an enemy. I know of no more shattering feeling than the knowledge of universal 'egoism', of the adult's ruthless pursuit of goals, that is commonly apt to dawn upon a young mind when it has completed its years of schooling. The more happily gifted a person is, the later he acquires this knowledge, which in intercourse with men constrains instinctive, playful action and turns it into laborious work, with all its vicissitudes and disappointments. But he who possesses the capacity for eternal youth, whom the years cannot age, remains capable also of a joyous supreme virtue, the generous virtue that does the good laughingly and scatters its gifts freely, instead of selling them for the consciousness of duty.

The higher ethos, the upper level of ethical life, is marked by strength and depth of feeling. And these, too, are at their greatest in the freshness of youth; indifference and obtuseness are sure signs of a soul grown old. The days of youth are in fact the period of deepest feelings, the time at which powerful impressions work most strongly on the heart, and everyone becomes a poet. This is undervalued for the most part, since at that time the feelings, for all their depth, are also more readily prone to alter and fly away; but anyone who in later years, when feelings are apt to be more persistent and lasting, can retain the strength of youthful sensations, will also find the ethical value of life deepened to ultimate felicity. And will discover that here, too, he attains the supreme meaning of existence only if he holds on to his youth.

The affirmation of youth as the true meaning of existence can be seen from a further viewpoint, which I might almost call a metaphysical one. Wherever we look in the world, we find everything in the grip of development, that is, in a process which successively traverses various characteristic phases. Living things, such as plants and animals, and inanimate things also, such as star-systems and atoms, develop and run through a variety of stages, which can well be called phases of youth and age. A plant grows and becomes a tree, the tree blossoms and bears fruit, and from the fruit springs a new tree that blossoms and bears fruit—where is the meaning in this cycle? The gardener who cultivates the tree will say: the meaning lies in the fruit, for that is why I tend the tree, and the blossom exists only for the sake of the fruit. But that is just his point of view. The poet, no less competent, will seek the meaning rather in the blossom, unfolding in its fragrance and beauty. And anyone who finds the highest meaning of existence in youth will be inclined to agree with the poet, and view the fruit as if it existed only so that new trees might grow from it, which will then in turn bloom and clothe themselves in a new abundance of beauty. The blossom in fact bears its value in itself, and this value is realized even if the fruit should happen to come to nothing. For the philosopher, however, the fruit likewise is its own purpose, and has its own beauty, its own youth, and in the life of a plant the different phases each have a meaning inherent in themselves.

It has often been denied that any sort of meaning is yet to be found in a cycle as such; a meaning enters only if the successive developments from blossom to fruit are in truth by no means alike; if, by virtue of the law of development, the fruits of each succeeding generation are finer and more perfect than those of the preceding one. The particular existence of the individual acquires a meaning only insofar as it contributes to the higher development of the species. Even the philosophy of history has mostly been based on this idea, though always, of course, with total lack of success. Does it not also seem, however, to have been an idea of Nietzsche's? Did he not also find the meaning of human existence in the fact that it is creating something above itself, that it is bringing forth the superman, and thus a higher being than man himself? If the doctrine had to be taken in this fashion, it would represent a contradiction of the Nietzschean viewpoint outlined earlier, and we should obviously have fallen into the same old error of transposing the meaning of existence out of itself and into the future. We would arrive at no true meaning, for the question would inevitably keep on arising again. Where, after all, would be the meaning of the superman's life? Would it not have to be sought in a super-superman, and so on? No, it is a serious though common misunderstanding of the idea of development, if we seek its meaning merely at the end, in the goal. It must lie, rather, in the process of self-development as such, in the proceeding, occurrence or activity itself; development does not lead to a final goal, but is itself the goal. We therefore arrive back at our major principle.

On cursory inspection, to be sure, the first period in the organism's development, youth in the biological sense, seems to be merely a preparation for the later years, merely a means to their purpose. But here, undoubtedly, it is just as in other cases of the kind: what at first was a mere means, develops into an end-in-itself, in that its intrinsic value is discovered. Nature finds pleasure in its own play, and seeks to prolong and draw it out, and it now evolves for its own sake. Thus the word is elaborated into verse, speaking into singing, walking into dancing, youth in the biological sense into youth in the philosophical sense. And the higher we ascend in the animal kingdom, the larger the portion of life that youth extends over. Even of man it is generally true, that the higher the level of racial development, the later the boy becomes a man, or the girl a woman.

Our whole culture will have to be focussed on a rejuvenation of man, rejuvenation in the philosophical sense, that all our doings become increasingly liberated from the domination of purposes, that even the actions necessary for life are turned into play. In many creatures this happens circuitously, in that youth in the purely biological sense is first extended over the whole of life, so that it turns into one long ascent which concludes at death, while the descent into old age is abolished as an unmeaning, obstructive arrangement. Such is the case with those wonderful plants, which bloom but once and then die, or with the bees, of whom the male consummates the act of mating with his death. Perhaps it can be achieved in man by a more direct route, as the sun of a brighter culture disperses the dark clouds of purpose, and the playful and youthful element, to which man is everywhere strongly disposed, emerges into the light of day.

All education should take care that nothing of the child in man is lost as he matures, that the separation of adolescence from adulthood is increasingly obliterated, so that the man remains a boy until his last years, and the woman a girl, in spite of being a mother. If we need a rule of life, let it be this: 'Preserve the spirit of youth!' For it is the meaning of life.

16

Ludwig Wittgenstein, "The Meaning of Life . . . We Can Call God," from *Notebooks 1914–1916*

Ludwig Wittgenstein (1889–1951), the author of the Tractatus Logico-Philosophicus *and the* Philosophical Investigations, *is thought by some to be the greatest philosopher of the twentieth century.*

11.6.16.

What do I know about God and the purpose of life?

I know that this world exists.

That I am placed in it like my eye in its visual field.

That something about it is problematic, which we call its meaning.

That this meaning does not lie in it but outside it. [*Cf.* 6.41.]

That life is the world. [*Cf.*5.621.]

That my will penetrates the world.

That my will is good or evil.

Therefore that good and evil are somehow connected with the meaning of the world.

The meaning of life, i.e. the meaning of the world, we can call God.

And connect with this the comparison of God to a father.

To pray is to think about the meaning of life.

I cannot bend the happenings of the world to my will: I am completely powerless.

I can only make myself independent of the world—and so in a certain sense master it—by renouncing any influence on happenings.

5.7.16.

The world is independent of my will. [6.373.]

Ludwig Wittgenstein, *Notebooks 1914–1916*, Oxford, Blackwell, 1979, pp. 72e–79e. Bracketed references are to the *Tractatus Logico-Philosophicus*, ed. G.H. von Wright and G.E.M. Anscombe.

Even if everything that we want were to happen, this would still only be, so to speak, a grace of fate, for what would guarantee it is not any logical connexion between will and world, and we could not in turn will the supposed physical connexion. [6.374.]

If good or evil willing affects the world it can only affect the boundaries of the world, not the facts, what cannot be portrayed by language but can only be shewn in language. [*Cf.* 6.43.]

In short, it must make the world a wholly different one. [*See* 6.43.]

The world must, so to speak, wax or wane as a whole. As if by accession or loss of meaning. [*Cf.* 6.43.]

As in death, too, the world does not change but stops existing. [6.431.]

6.7.16.

And in this sense Dostoievsky is right when he says that the man who is happy is fulfilling the purpose of existence.

Or again we could say that the man is fulfilling the purpose of existence who no longer needs to have any purpose except to live. That is to say, who is content.

For life in the present there is no death.

Death is not an event in life. It is not a fact of the world. [*Cf.* 6.4311.]

If by eternity is understood not infinite temporal duration but non-temporality, then it can be said that a man lives eternally if he lives in the present. [*See* 6.4311.]

In order to live happily I must be in agreement with the world. And that is what "being happy" *means*.

I am then, so to speak, in agreement with that alien will on which I appear dependent. That is to say: 'I am doing the will of God'.

Fear in face of death is the best sign of a false, i.e.-a bad, life.

When my conscience upsets my equilibrium, then I am not in agreement with Something. But what is this? Is it *the world*?

Certainly it is correct to say: Conscience is the voice of God.

For example: it makes me unhappy to think that I have offended such and such a man. Is that my conscience?

Can one say: "Act according to your conscience whatever it may be"?

Live happy!

. . .

Man cannot make himself happy without more ado.

Whoever lives in the present lives without fear and hope.

21.7.16.
What really is the situation of the human will? I will call "will" first and foremost the bearer of good and evil.

Let us imagine a man who could use none of his limbs and hence could, in the ordinary sense, not exercise his *will*. He could, however, think and *want* and communicate his thoughts to someone else. Could therefore do good or evil through the other man. Then it is clear that ethics would have validity for him, too, and that he in the *ethical sense* is the bearer of a *will*.

Now is there any difference in principle between this will and that which sets the human body in motion?

Or is the mistake here this: even *wanting* (thinking) is an activity of the will? (And in this sense, indeed, a man *without* will would not be alive.)

But can we conceive a being that isn't capable of Will at all, but only of Idea (of seeing for example)? In some sense this seems impossible. But if it were possible then there could also be a world without ethics.

24.7.16.
The World and Life are one. [5.621.]

Physiological life is of course not "Life". And neither is psychological life. Life is the world.

Ethics does not treat of the world. Ethics must be a condition of the world, like logic.

Ethics and aesthetics are one. [*See* 6.421.]

29.7.16.

For it is a fact of logic that wanting does not stand in any logical connexion with its own fulfilment. And it is also clear that the world of the happy is a *different* world from the world of the unhappy. [*Cf.* 6.43.]

Is seeing an activity?

Is it possible to will good, to will evil, and not to will?

Or is only he happy who does *not* will?

"To love one's neighbour" would mean to will!

But can one want and yet not be unhappy if the want does not attain fulfilment? (And this possibility always exists.)

Is it, according to common conceptions, good to want *nothing* for one's neighbour, neither good nor evil?

And yet in a certain sense it seems that not wanting is the only good.

Here I am still making crude mistakes! No doubt of that!

It is generally assumed that it is evil to want someone else to be unfortunate. Can this be correct? Can it be worse than to want him to be fortunate?

Here everything seems to turn, so to speak, on *how* one wants.

It seems one can't say anything more than: Live happily!

The world of the happy is a different world from that of the unhappy. [*See* 6.43.]

The world of the happy is *a happy world*.

Then can there be a world that is neither happy nor unhappy?

30.7.16.

When a general ethical law of the form "Thou shalt . . . " is set up, the first thought is: Suppose I do not do it?

But it is clear that ethics has nothing to do with punishment and reward. So this question about the consequences of an action must be unimportant. At least these consequences cannot be events. For there must be something right about that question after all. There must be a *kind* of ethical reward and of ethical punishment but these must be involved in the action itself.

And it is also clear that the reward must be something pleasant, the punishment something unpleasant.

[6.422.]

I keep on coming back to this! simply the happy life is good, the unhappy bad. And if I *now* ask myself: But why should I live *happily*, then this of itself seems to me to be a tautological question; the happy life seems to be justified, of itself, it seems that it *is* the only right life.

But this is really in some sense deeply mysterious! *It is clear* that ethics *cannot* be expressed! [*Cf.* 6.421.]

But we could say: The happy life seems to be in some sense more *harmonious* than the unhappy. But in what sense??

What is the objective mark of the happy, harmonious life? Here it is again clear that there cannot be any such mark, that can be *described*.

This mark cannot be a physical one but only a metaphysical one, a transcendental one.

Ethics is transcendental. [*See* 6.421.]

1.8.16.

How things stand, is God.

God is, how things stand.

Only from the consciousness of the *uniqueness of my life* arises religion—science—and art.

2.8.16.

And this consciousness is life itself.

Can there by any ethics if there is no living being but myself?

If ethics is supposed to be something fundamental, there can.

If I am right, then it is not sufficient for the ethical judgment that a world is given.

Then the world in itself is neither good nor evil.

For it must be all one, as far as concerns the existence of ethics, whether there is living matter in the world or not. And it is clear that a world in which there is only dead matter is in itself neither good nor evil, so even the world of living things can in itself be neither good nor evil.

Good and evil only enter through the *subject*. And the subject is not part of the world, but a boundary of the world. [*Cf.* 5.632.]

It would be possible to say (à la Schopenhauer): It is not the world of Idea that is either good or evil; but the willing subject.

I am conscious of the complete unclarity of all these sentences.

Going by the above, then, the willing subject would have to be happy or unhappy, and happiness and unhappiness could not be part of the world.

As the subject is not a part of the world but a presupposition of its existence, so good and evil which are predicates of the subject, are not properties in the world.

Here the nature of the subject is completely veiled.

My work has extended from the foundations of logic to the nature of the world.

17

Leo Nikolaevich Tolstoy, "The Fundamental Contradiction of Human Life" and "The Fear of Death Is Only a Confession of the Unsolved Contradiction of Life," from *Life*

Count Leo Nikolaevich Tolstoy (1828–1910), the great Russian novelist, wrote Anna Karenina *and* War and Peace, *and as well* What Is Art? *and numerous philosophical and religious writings arguing for a very pure ethical version of Christianity.*

The Fundamental Contradiction of Human Life

Every man lives only for his own good, for his personal welfare. If man feels no desire for happiness, he is not even conscious that he is alive. Man cannot imagine life without the desire for happiness. To live is, for every man, the same thing as to desire and to attain bliss; to desire and to attain bliss is synonymous with living. Man is conscious of life only in himself, only in his own personality, and hence, at first, man imagines that the bliss which he desires for himself personally is happiness, and nothing more.

At first, it seems to him that he is truly alive, and he alone.

The life of other beings seems to him not in the least like his own. He imagines it as merely the semblance of life. Man only observes the life of other beings, and learns from observation only that they are alive. Man knows about the life of other beings when he is willing to think of them, but he knows of his own, he cannot for a single moment cease to be conscious that he lives, and hence real life appears to every man as his own life only, while the life of other beings about him seems to him to be merely a condition of his own existence. If he does not

Tolstoy, *Life*, Walter Scott, London, no date.

desire evil to others, it is only because the sight of the sufferings of others interferes with his happiness. If he desires good to others, it is not at all the same as for himself—it is not in order that the person to whom he wishes good may be well placed, but only in order that the happiness of other beings may augment the welfare of his own life. Only that happiness in this life is important and necessary to a man which he feels to be his own, i.e., his own individual happiness.

And behold, in striving for the attainment of this, his own individual welfare, man perceives that his welfare depends upon other beings. And, upon watching and observing these other beings, man sees that all of them, both men and even animals, possess precisely the same conception of life as he himself. Each one of these beings, precisely as in his own case, is conscious only of his own life, and his own happiness, considers his own life alone of importance, and real, and the life of all other beings only as a means to his individual welfare. Man sees that every living being, precisely like himself, must be ready, for the sake of his petty welfare, to deprive all other beings of greater happiness and even of life.

And, having comprehended this, man involuntarily makes this calculation, that if this is so, and he knows that it is indubitably so, then, not one or not ten beings only, but all the innumerable beings in the world, for the attainment, each of his own object, are ready every moment to annihilate him, that man for whom alone life exists. And, having apprehended this, man sees that his personal happiness, in which alone he understands life, is not only not to be easily won by him, but that it will assuredly be taken from him.

The longer a man lives, the more firmly is this conviction confirmed by experience, and the man perceives that the life of the world in which he shares is composed of individualities bound together, desirous of exterminating and devouring each other, not only cannot be a happiness for him, but will, assuredly, be a great evil.

But, nevertheless, if the man is placed in such favorable conditions that he can successfully contend with other personalities, fearing nothing for his own, both experience and reason speedily show him, that even those semblances of happiness which he wrests from life, in the form of enjoyment for his personality, do not constitute happiness, and are but specimens of happiness as it were, vouchsafed him merely in order that he may be the more vividly conscious of the suffering which is always bound up with enjoyment.

The longer man lives, the more plainly does he see that weariness, satiety, toils, and sufferings become ever greater and greater, and enjoyments ever less and less.

But this is not all. On beginning to become conscious of a decline of strength, and of ill-health, and gazing upon ill-health, age, and the death of others, he perceives this also in addition, that even his existence, in which alone he recognizes real, full life, is approaching weakness, old age, and death, with every hour, with every movement; that his life, besides being subject to thousands of chances of annihilation from other beings warring with him, and from ever increasing sufferings, is, in virtue of its very nature, nothing else than an incessant approach to death; to that condition in which together with the life of the individual will, assuredly, be annihilated every possibility of any personal happiness. The man perceives that he, his own personality, is that in which alone he feels life, that all he does is to struggle with those with whom it is impossible to struggle—with the whole world; that he is in search of enjoyments which give only the semblances of happiness, and which always terminate in sufferings, and he wishes to hold back life, which it is impossible to hold back. The man perceives that he himself, his own personality, that for which, alone, he desires life and happiness, can have neither life nor happiness. And that which he desires to have—life and happiness—is possessed only by those beings who are strangers to him, whom he does not feel, and cannot feel, and of whose existence he cannot know and does not wish to know.

That which for him is the most important of all, and which alone is necessary to him, that which—as it seems to him—alone possesses life in reality, his personality, that which will perish, will become bones and worms, is not he; but that which is unnecessary for him, unimportant to him, all that world of ever changing and struggling beings, that is to say, real life, will remain, and will exist forever. So that the sole life which is felt by man, and which evokes all this activity, proves to be something deceptive and impossible; but the inward life, which he does not love, which he does not feel, of which he is ignorant, is the one real life.

That of which he is not conscious—that alone possesses those qualities of which he would fain be the sole possessor. And this is not that which presents itself to a man in the evil moments of his gloomy moods, this is not a representation which it is possible for him not to have, but this is, on the contrary, such a palpable, indubitable truth, that if this thought once occurs to man, or if others explain it to him, he can never again free himself from it, he can never more force it out of his consciousness.

The Sole Aim of Life[1]

The sole aim of life, as it first presents itself to man, is the happiness of himself as an individual, but individual happiness there cannot be; if there were anything resembling individual happiness in life, then that life in which alone happiness can exist, the life of the individual, is borne irresistibly, by every moment, by every breath, towards suffering, towards evil, towards death, towards annihilation.

And this is so self-evident and so plain that every thinking man, old or young, learned or unlearned, will see it.

This argument is so simple and natural that it presents itself to every reasoning man, and has been known to mankind ever since the most ancient times.

"The life of man as an individual, striving only towards his own happiness, amid an endless number of similar individuals, engaged in annihilating each other and in annihilating themselves, is evil and absurdity, and such real life cannot be." This is what man has been saying to himself from the most ancient times down to the present day, and this inward inconsistency of the life of man was expressed with remarkable force and clearness by the Indians, and the Chinese, and the Egyptians, and the Greeks, and the Jews, and from the most ancient times the mind of man has been directed to the study of such a happiness for man as should not be cancelled by the contest of beings among themselves, by suffering and by death. In the increasingly better solution of this indubitable, unavoidable contest, by sufferings and by death of the happiness of man, lies the constant movement in advance from that time when we know his life.

From the most ancient times, and among the most widely varying peoples, the great teachers of mankind have revealed to men more and more the clear definitions of life, solving its inward contradictions, and have pointed out the true happiness and true life which is proper to men.

And, since the position of all men in the world is identical, since the contradictions of his strivings after his personal welfare and the consciousness of his powerlessness are identical for every man, all the definitions of true happiness of life, and, hence, of the true revelation to men by the grandest minds of humanity, are identical.

---

1. The contradiction of life has been known to mankind from the most ancient times. The enlighteners of mankind expounded to men the definition of life, resolving it into an inward contradiction, but the Scribes and Pharisees conceal it from the people.

"Life is the diffusion of that light which, for the happiness of men, descended upon them from heaven," said Confucius, six hundred years before Christ.

"Life is the peregrination and the perfection of souls, which attain to greater and ever greater bliss," said the Brahmins of the same day.

"Life is the abnegation of self, with the purpose of attaining blessed Nirvana," said Buddha, a contemporary of Confucius.

"Life is the path of peacefulness and lowliness, for the attainment of bliss," said Loa-dzi, also a contemporary of Confucius.

"Life is that which God breathed into man's nostrils, in order that he, by fulfilling his law, might receive happiness," says the Hebrew sage, Moses.

"Life is submission to the reason, which gives happiness to man," said the Stoics.

"Life is love towards God and our neighbor, which gives happiness to man," said Christ, summing up in his definition all those which had preceded it.

Such are the definitions of life, which, thousands of years before our day, pointing out to men real and indestructible bliss, in the place of the false and impossible bliss of individuality, solve the contradictions of human life and impart to it a reasonable sense.

It is possible not to agree with these definitions of life, it is possible to assume that these definitions can be expressed more accurately and more clearly; but it is impossible not to see that these definitions, equally with the acknowledgment of them, do away with the inconsistencies of life, and, replacing the aspiration for an unattainable bliss of individuality, by another aspiration, for a happiness indestructible by suffering and death, impart to life a reasonable sense. It is impossible not to see this also, that these definitions, being theoretically correct, are confirmed by the experience of life, and that millions and millions of men, who have accepted and who do accept such definitions of life, have, in fact, proved, and do prove, the possibility of replacing the aspiration towards individual welfare by an aspiration towards another happiness, of a sort which is not to be destroyed by suffering or death.

But, in addition to those men who have understood and who do understand the definitions of life, revealed to men by the great enlighteners of humanity, and who live by them, there always have been and there are now many people who, during a certain period of their life, and sometimes their whole life long, lead a purely animal existence, not only ignoring those definitions which serve to solve the contradictions of human life, but not even perceiving those contradictions which they solve. And there always have been and there now exist among those people men who, in consequence of their exclusively external position, regard themselves as called upon to guide mankind, and who, without themselves comprehending the meaning of human life, have taught and do teach other people life, which they themselves do not understand; to the effect that human life is nothing but individual existence.

Such false teachers have existed in all ages, and exist in our day also. Some confess in words the teachings of those enlighteners of mankind, in whose traditions they have been brought up, but, not comprehending their rational meaning, they convert these teachings into supernatural revelations as to the past and future life of men, and require only the fulfillment of ceremonial forms.

This is the doctrine of the Pharisees, in the very broadest sense, i.e., of the men who teach that a life preposterous in itself can be amended by faith in a future life, obtained by the fulfillment of external forms.

Others, who do not acknowledge the possibility of any other life than the visible one, reject every marvel and everything supernatural, and boldly affirm that the life of man is nothing but his animal existence from his birth to his death. This is the doctrine of the Scribes—of men who teach that there is nothing preposterous in the life of man, any more than in that of animals.

And both the former and the latter false prophets, in spite of the fact that the teaching of both is founded upon the same coarse lack of understanding of the fundamental inconsistency of human life, have always been at enmity with each other, and are still at enmity. Both these doctrines reign in our world, and, contending with each other, they fill the world with their dissensions—by those same dissensions concealing from men those definitions of life which reveal the path to the true happiness of men, and which were given to men thousands of years ago.

The Pharisees, not comprehending this definition of life, which was given to men by those teachers in whose traditions they were brought up, replace it with their false interpretations of a future life, and, in addition to this, strive to conceal from men the definition of life of other enlighteners of humanity, by presenting the latter to their disciples in the coarsest and harshest aspect, assuming that, by so doing, they will uphold the absolute authority of that doctrine upon which they found their interpretation.[2]

And the Scribes, not even suspecting in the teachings of the Pharisees those intelligent grounds from which they took their rise, flatly reject all doctrines, and boldly affirm that all these doctrines have no foundation whatever, but are merely remnants of the coarse customs of ignorance, and that the forward movement of mankind consists in not putting any questions whatever to one's self, concerning life, which overleap the bounds of the animal existence of man.

The Fear of Death is Only a Confession of the Unsolved Contradiction of Life

"There is no death," the voice of truth says to men. "I am the Resurrection and the Life; he that believeth in Me, though he were dead, yet shall he live. And every one that liveth and believeth in Me shall never die. Believest thou this?"

"There is no death," say all the great teachers of the world; and the same say millions of men who understand life, and bear witness to it with their lives. And every living man feels the same thing in his soul, at the moment when his consciousness clears up. But men who do not understand life cannot do otherwise than fear death. They see it, and believe in it.

"How is there no death?" cry these people in wrath and indignation. "This is sophistry! Death is before us; it has mowed down millions, and it will mow us down as well. And you may say as much as you please that it does not exist, it will remain all the same. Yonder it is!"

And they see that of which they speak, as a man mentally afflicted sees the vision which terrifies him. He cannot handle the vision, it has never touched him; of its intentions he knows nothing, but he is alarmed, and he suffers from this imaginary vision, which is deprived of the possibility of life. And it is the same with death. Man does not know his death, and never can know it; it has never yet touched him, of its intentions he knows nothing. Then what is it that he fears?

"It has never yet seized me, but it will seize me, that I surely know—

2. The unity of the rational idea of the definition of life by other enlighteners of mankind does not present itself to them as proof of the truth of their teaching, since it injures faith in the senseless, false interpretations with which they replace the substance of doctrine.

it will seize me and annihilate me. And that is terrible," say men who do not understand life.

If men with false ideas of life could reason calmly, and think accurately on the basis of that conception which they have of life, they would be forced to the conclusion that in what is produced in my fleshly existence by the change which I see proceeding, incessantly, in all beings, and which I call death, there is nothing disagreeable or terrible.

I shall die. What is there terrible about that? How many changes have taken place, and are now in progress, in my fleshly existence, and I have not feared them? Why should I fear this change which has not yet come, and in which there is not only nothing repulsive to my reason and experience, but which is so comprehensible, so familiar, and so natural for me, that during the whole course of my life I have formed fancies, I still form them, in which the death both of animals and of people has been accepted by me as a necessary and often an agreeable condition of life. What is there terrible about it?

For there are but two strictly logical views of life: one false—that by which life is understood as those seeming phenomena which take place in my body from my birth to my death; and another, the true one—by which life is understood as that invisible consciousness of it which I bear within myself. One view is false, the other is true; but both are logical, and men may hold either the one or the other, but in neither the one nor the other is the fear of death possible.

The first false view, which understands life as the visible phenomena in the body from birth to death, is as old as the world itself. This is not, as many think, a view of life which has been worked out by the materialistic science and philosophy of our day; the science and philosophy of our times have only carried this view to its extreme limits, by which it becomes more visible than hitherto how little this view corresponds to the fundamental demands of human life; but this is the ancient and primitive view of men who stood upon the lower steps of culture. It is expressed among the Chinese, among the Greeks, and among the Hebrews, in the Book of Job, and in the sentence: "Dust thou art, and to dust shalt thou return."

This view, in its present expression, runs as follows: Life is a chance play of forces in matter, manifesting itself in space and time. And what we call our consciousness is not life, but a certain delusion of the feelings, which makes it appear that life lies in this consciousness. Consciousness is the spark which flashes up from matter under certain conditions of the latter. This spark flashes up, burns, again grows feeble, and finally goes out. This spark, that is to say, consciousness, experienced by matter in the course of a certain time, between two endless spaces of time, is nothing. And, in spite of the fact that consciousness sees and passes judgment on itself and all the infinite world, and beholds all the play of chance of this world,—and *chief of all*, in the contrary something that is not accidental, calls this play accident,—this consciousness itself is only the product of dead matter, a vision, appearing and disappearing without any trace or reason. All is the product of matter, infinitely varied; and what is called life is only a certain condition of dead matter.

Such is one view of life. This view is utterly false. According to this view, the rational consciousness of man is merely an accident, accompanying a certain condition of matter; and therefore, what we, in our consciousness, call life, is a phantom. The dead only exists. What we call life is the play of death. With such a view of life, death should not only be terrible, but life ought to be terrible, as something unnatural and senseless, as it is among the Buddhists, and the new pessimists, Schopenhauer and Hartmann.

The other view of life is as follows. Life is only that which I recognize in myself. But I am always conscious of my life, not as I have been or as I shall be (thus I meditate upon my life), but I am conscious of my life thus—that I am—that I never begin anywhere, that I shall never end anywhere. No comprehension of time and space is connected with my consciousness of life. My life is manifested in time, in space, but this is merely its manifestation. But the life itself of which I am conscious makes itself perceptible to me outside of time and space; so that, according to this view, it appears, not that the consciousness of life is a phantom, but all that which is dependent upon space and is visionary in time.

And, therefore, a curtailment of the bodily existence, so far as connected with time and space, has nothing wretched about it, according to this view, and can neither shorten nor destroy my true life. And, according to this view, death does not exist.

There could be no fear of death according to either view of life, if men held strictly to either the one or the other.

Neither as an animal, nor as a rational being, can man fear death; the animal has no consciousness of life and does not see death, and the rational being, having a consciousness of life, cannot see in the death of the animal anything except a natural and never ending movement of matter. But if man fears, what he fears is not death, which he does not know, but life, which alone he does know, and his animal and rational existence. That feeling which is expressed in men by the fear of death is only the consciousness of the inward contradiction of life; just as the fear of ghosts is merely a consciousness of a sickly mental condition.

"I shall cease to be, I shall die, all that in which I set my life will die," says one voice to a man.

"I am," says another voice, "and I cannot die, and I ought not to die. I ought not to die, and I am dying."

Not in death, but in this contradiction lies the cause of that terror which seizes upon a man, at the thought of death of the flesh: the fear of death lies not in the fact that man dreads the curtailment of his animal existence, but in the fact that it seems to him that that will die which cannot and must not die. The thought of future death is only a transference to the future of the death which takes place in the present. The phantom which presents itself of a future death of the flesh is not an awakening of the thought of death, but, on the contrary, an awakening of the thought of the life which a man should have and which he has not.

This feeling is similar to that which a man would experience on awaking to life in his grave, under ground. "There is life, but I am in death, and here it is, death!" He imagines that what is and must be will be annihilated. And the mind of man mourns and grows afraid. The best proof of the fact that the fear of death is not the fear of death, but of false life, is this, that men frequently kill themselves from the fear of death.

Men are not terrified by the thought of the death of the flesh because they are afraid that their life will end with it, but because the death of the flesh plainly demonstrates to them the necessity of a true life, which they do not possess. And this is why people who do not understand life are so disinclined to think of death. To think of death is exactly the same with them as to confess that they are not living as their rational consciousness demands.

People who fear death, fear it because it represents emptiness and darkness to them; but they behold emptiness and darkness because they do not see life.

18

Simone Weil, "Detachment," from *Gravity and Grace*

Simone Weil (1909–1943), French philosopher and political writer, was an authentic modern mystic. Gravity and Grace *contains her most important thoughts.*

Affliction in itself is not enough for the attainment of total detachment. Unconsoled affliction is necessary. There must be no consolation—no apparent consolation. Ineffable consolation then comes down.

To forgive debts. To accept the past without asking for future compensation. To stop time at the present instant. This is also the acceptance of death.

'He emptied himself of his divinity.' To empty ourselves of the world. To take the form of a slave. To reduce ourselves to the point we occupy in space and time—that is to say, to nothing.

To strip ourselves of the imaginary royalty of the world. Absolute solitude. Then we possess the truth of the world.

Two ways of renouncing material possessions:
To give them up with a view to some spiritual advantage.

To conceive of them and feel them as conducive to spiritual well-being (for example: hunger, fatigue and humiliation cloud the mind and hinder meditation) and yet to renounce them.

Only the second kind of renunciation means nakedness of spirit.

Furthermore, material goods would scarcely be dangerous if they were seen in isolation and not bound up with spiritual advantage.

We must give up everything which is not grace and not even desire grace.

The extinction of desire (Buddhism)—or detachment—or *amor fati*—or desire for the absolute good—these all amount to the same: to empty desire, finality of all content, to desire in the void, to desire without any wishes.

To detach our desire from all good things and to wait. Experience proves that this waiting is satisfied. It is then we touch the absolute good.

Always, beyond the particular object whatever it may be, we have to fix our will on the void—to will the void. For the good which we can neither picture nor define is a void for us. But this void is fuller than all fullnesses.

If we get as far as this we shall come through all right, for God fills the void. It has nothing to do with an intellectual process in the present-day sense. The intelligence has nothing to discover, it has only to clear the ground. It is only good for servile tasks.

The good seems to us as a nothingness, since there is no *thing* that is good. But this nothingness is not unreal. Compared with it, everything in existence is unreal.

We must leave on one side the beliefs which fill up voids and sweeten what is bitter. The belief in immortality. The belief in the utility of sin: *etiam peccata*. The belief in the providential ordering of events— in short the 'consolations' which are ordinarily sought in religion.

To love God through and across the destruction of Troy and of Carthage—and with no consolation. Love is not consolation, it is light.

The reality of the world is the result of our attachment. It is the reality of the self which we transfer into things. It has nothing to do with independent reality. That is only perceptible through total detachment. Should only one thread remain, there is still attachment.

Affliction which forces us to attach ourselves to the most wretched objects exposes in all its misery the true character of attachment. In this way the necessity for detachment is made more obvious.

Attachment is a manufacturer of illusions and whoever wants reality ought to be detached.

As soon as we know that something is real we can no longer be attached to it.

Attachment is no more nor less than an insufficiency in our sense of reality. We are attached to the possession of a thing because we think that if we cease to possess it, it will cease to exist. A great many people do not feel with their whole soul that there is all the difference in the world between the destruction of a town and their own irremediable exile from that town.

Human misery would be intolerable if it were not diluted in time. We have to prevent it from being diluted *in order that it should* be intolerable.

'And when they had had their fill of tears' (*Iliad*).—This is another way of making the worst suffering bearable.

We must not weep so that we may not be comforted.

All suffering which does not detach us is wasted suffering. Nothing is more frightful, a desolate coldness, a warped soul (Ovid. Slaves in Plautus).

Never to think of a thing or being we love but have not actually before our eyes without reflecting that perhaps this thing has been destroyed, or this person is dead.

May our sense of reality not be dissolved by this thought but made more intense.

Each time that we say 'Thy will be done' we should have in mind all possible misfortunes added together.

Two ways of killing ourselves: suicide or detachment.

To kill by our thought everything we love: the only way to die. Only what we love, however ('He who hateth not his father and mother . . .' but: 'Love your enemies . . .').

Not to desire that what we love should be immortal. We should neither desire the immortality nor the death of any human being, whoever he may be, with whom we have to do.

The miser deprives himself of his treasure because of his desire for it. If we can let our whole good rest with something hidden in the ground, why not with God?

But when God has become as full of significance as the treasure is for the miser, we have to tell ourselves insistently that he does not exist. We must experience the fact that we love him, even if he does not exist.

It is he who, through the operation of the dark night, withdraws himself in order not to be loved like the treasure is by the miser.

Electra weeping for the dead Orestes. If we love God while thinking that he does not exist, he will manifest his existence.

19

William Shakespeare, "Fear No More. . . ."
from *Cymbeline*

Williamn Shakespeare (1564–1616), English playwright, was born in Stratford-upon-Avon and lived mostly in London, where he was a member of a company of actors and was involved in the direction of his own plays.

	Song.
GUIDERIUS.	Fear no more the heat o' th' sun,
	Nor the furious winter's rages;
	Thou thy worldly task hast done,
	Home art gone, and ta'en thy wages:
	Golden lads and girls all must,
	As chimney-sweepers, come to dust.
ARVIRAGUS.	Fear no more the frown o' the great,
	Thou art past the tyrant's stroke;
	Care no more to clothe and eat;
	To thee the reed is as the oak:
	The sceptre, learning, physic, must
	All follow this, and come to dust.
GUIDERIUS.	Fear no more the lightning-flash,
ARVIRAGUS.	Nor th' all-dreaded thunder-stone;
GUIDERIUS.	Fear not slander, censure rash;
ARVIRAGUS.	Thou hast finisht joy and moan:
BOTH.	All lovers young, all lovers must,
	Consign to thee, and come to dust.
GUIDERIUS.	No exorciser harm thee!
ARVIRAGUS.	Nor no witchcraft charm thee!

GUIDERIUS.   Ghost unlaid forbear thee.

ARVIRAGUS.   Nothing ill come near thee.

BOTH.   Quiet consummation have.
And renowned be thy grave.

Some Suggested Further Reading

Bell, Richard H., *Simone Weil's Philosophy of Culture: Readings Toward a Divine Humanity*, Cambridge, Cambridge University Press, 1993.

Dilman, Ilham, "Life and Meaning", *Philosophy*, 40 (1965).

Findlay, J.N., *Plato: the Written and the Unwritten Doctrine*, New York, Humanities Press, 1974.

Gilson, Étienne, *The Christian Philosophy of St. Augustine*, New York, Random House, 1960.

Heidegger, Martin, *Being and Time* trans. J. Macquarrie and Edward Robinson, New York, Harper and Row, 1962, Ch. I, Division II, "Dascin's Possibility of Being-A-Whole and Being Towards Death".

Kaufman, Walter, *Nietzsche: Philosopher, Psychologist, Anti-Christ*, Princeton, Princeton University Press, 1950.

Klemke, E.D., ed., *The Meaning of Life*, Oxford, Oxford University Press, 1981.

Levenson, Carl, "Distance and Presence in Augustine's *Confessions*", *Journal of Religion*, (1984).

Nagel, Thomas, *The View From Nowhere*, Oxford, Oxford University Press, 1986, Ch. XI, "Birth, Death and the Meaning of Life".

———, *What Does It All Mean? A Very Short Introduction to Philosophy*, Oxford, Oxford University Press, 1987, Chapters 9 and 10.

Nussbaum, Martha, *The Fragility of Goodness*, Cambridge, Cambridge University Press, 1986, esp. Part II.

Ricoeur, Paul, *Fallible Man* trans. Charles Kelby, Chicago, Henry Regnery, 1965.

Russell, L.J., "The Meaning of Life", *Philosophy*, 28 (1953).

Sanders, Steven and Cheney, David R., *The Meaning of Life: Questions, Answers, Analysis*, Englewood, Prentice Hall, 1980.

Sartre, Jean-Paul, "Camus' The Outsider" in *Literary and Philosophical Essays*, New York, Collier, 1962.

———, "Reply to Camus" and "Albert Camus" in *Situations*, New York, Fawcett Crest, New York, 1966.

Sheridan, James, *Once More from the Middle: A Philosophical Anthropology*, Athens, Ohio, University of Ohio Press, 1973.

Sprague, Rosamond Kent, *Plato's Philosopher-King*, Columbia, University of South Carolina Press, 1976.

Taylor, Richard, *Good and Evil*, New York, Macmillan, 1970, Ch. 18.

Teselle, Eugene, *Augustine the Theologian*, London, Burns and Oates, 1976.

Tolstoy, Leo, *My Confession*, trans. Leo Wiener, London, Dent, 1905.

——, "The Death of Ivan Illich", trans. Louise and Aylmer Maude, in *Great Short Works of Leo Tolstoy*. New York, 1967.

Wiggins, David, "Truth, Invention and the Meaning of Life", Essay III of *Needs, Values and Truth*, Oxford, Blackwell, 1991.

Wittgenstein, Ludwig, *Tractatus Logico-Philosophicus*, trans. D.F. Pears and B.F. McGuinness, London, Routledge, 1961, 6.4–7.

Index